SOCIAL RULES!
FOR ENTREPRENEURS AND SMALL BUSINESS

A Common Sense Guide to Social Media Marketing

PAUL SLACK

Social Rules! For Entrepreneurs and Small Business: A Common Sense Guide to Social Media Marketing

Copyright © 2012 Paul Slack. All rights reserved. No part of this book may be reproduced or retransmitted in any form or by any means without the written permission of the publisher.

Published by Wheatmark®
1760 East River Road, Suite 145, Tucson, Arizona 85718 U.S.A.
www.wheatmark.com

ISBN: 978-1-60494-798-4
LCCN: 2012935992

I dedicate this book to the man behind the curtain, Marc Sparks.

Without his dedication to faith, passion, tenacity, focus, monetization, and an outrageous sense of urgency, this book would have never happened.

TABLE OF CONTENTS

Foreword by Darren Hardy — vii
Acknowledgement — xi
Introduction — xiii

PART 1: NEW RULES OF MARKETING — 1

Chapter 1   The Rules Have Changed — 3
Chapter 2   What Is Social Media Marketing? — 15
Chapter 3   Additional Benefits To Social Media Marketing — 23
Chapter 4   Social Media Marketing=Search Engine Optimization 2.0 — 37
Chapter 5   Social Media Strategy — 45
Chapter 6   Rules of Engagement — 63

PART 2: THE TACTICAL WHEEL — 75

Chapter 7   Listening — 79
Chapter 8   Building Community — 89
Chapter 9   Broadcasting — 99
Chapter 10   Developing Content — 109
Chapter 11   Conversion — 121

PART 3: SOCIAL MEDIA PLATFORMS — 133

Chapter 12   Facebook — 135
Chapter 13   Twitter — 159
Chapter 14   LinkedIn — 189
Chapter 15   YouTube — 213
Chapter 16   Blogs — 237
Chapter 17   Measuring Results — 257
Chapter 18   Tying It All Together — 275

Reference   SEO Tactics – The Secret Sauce — 287
Appendix — 311

FOREWORD

"Social Media Expert" Google it. More than 1 million pages come up in 0.42 seconds. Search "social media" on Amazon.com. You'll get a list of 172,339 recommended books. Perplexing isn't it? Who do you believe? Who is legitimate? What's the truth? What works in the real world of business? As Publisher and Editorial Director of SUCCESS magazine it is my job to investigate, vet and filter the pretenders from the genuine thought leaders in a variety of personal and professional success categories. I am writing this foreword because Paul Slack is the real deal and Social Rules! is a legitimate guidebook to finally help you discern and leverage this important marketing and communication platform referred to as "social media" (359 million pages on Google by the way).

Small strategic disciplines, executed every day, over time compound into extraordinary results. For true success, there's no magic bullet, no shortcut or quick fix. In my book, The Compound Effect, I demonstrate how small, seemingly insignificant changes can create huge differences in outcomes. The same is true for social media marketing. Signing up for a service to get 10,000 followers on Twitter will not create raving fans. Placing an ad on Facebook will not generate great wealth. Desire and motivation is not enough to succeed—particularly in social media. It takes the right tools and the right strategies to reap lasting and meaningful results. Paul Slack does an exceptional job of teaching the key strategic steps you can implement over time to create a significant and quantifiable revenue results. You'll learn the most effective strategies to maximize your efforts and connect the dots between social media tactics and real business growth.

Paul and I share the belief that consistency is the ultimate key to success. Social Rules! will give you the plan to make the right moves, in the right ways in the right places consistently. You will develop successful habits and gradually your efforts will be compounded. What once looked like an impossible goal (doubling or even tripling your revenues) will be achieved one consistent step at a time. It's what I call "Harnessing the Power of Big Mo." By using Paul's insights and applying steady effort you will benefit from the power of momentum. The Tactical Wheel Paul developed is one of the most clearly explained methods I've seen for developing strategic choices, habits and gaining "mo" with social media marketing.

If you want success, go about helping others obtain it. Using social media marketing for the sole purpose of pushing your own products will not bring you success; adding value to others with integrity will. Paul provides the blueprint for remarkable content to educate and inform your customer. You will build solid relationships with your clients that will lead to optimal professional and personal success for everyone. In the long run, what your customers learn from you through social media will be a much more powerful marketing strategy than any ad space you can purchase.

Measure your tangible results. It's true a new blog or post on Facebook may not immediately bring people to your bricks-and-mortar business, or have your online shopping cart working overtime. Nonetheless, there are ways to measure the effects of your efforts. Paul shows you how to track and monitor your results so you can recognize the origin of your wins and make adjustments when necessary.

Be the overseer, not the administrator. Social Rules! is not a step-by-step book for how to set up and administer accounts. It is a strategic marketing book for CEOs and business owners who want to know how to work smart, what to do, and how to do it. Paul walks you through all the available strategies and discusses how to appropriately optimize each for your business.

Learn what works and what doesn't—from the best in the business. For the past eighteen years, I've been a leader in the success industry. I've worked with respected thought leaders and I've mentored business leaders, corporate executives, and countless high-achievers. I know the incredible value of gaining access to expert advice and strategic guidance. Social Rules! can dramatically shorten your learning curve and save you tons of headache, heartache and wallet ache. It will show you how real professionals in real businesses are really moving the needle with this powerful new medium to attract, engage and retain fruitful new relationships that can dramatically expand your company's mission, influence and contribution in the marketplace.

Darren Hardy

- Publisher, SUCCESS magazine

- Author, The Compound Effect

ACKNOWLEDGEMENT

This book couldn't have been made possible without the help and support of some very important people in my life.

To my wife, Beth for her encouragement and patience while writing the book. Michael, Ryan, and Madeline, the three children God has blessed Beth and I with, for their perspective about ways to enjoy and use the internet.

To the Splash Media team for their diligence and dedication in offering tips and advice on the best ways to deliver social media to our clients. Thank you to Chris Kraft and Mark Hitchner, for their encouragement and insights.

To Ajit George, my client and dear friend. I imagined you every time I closed my eyes and thought about the type of business man who would benefit from the ideas expressed in these chapters.

Finally, to Christine Messier, my collaborative editor, for her commitment to excellence and making what could have been a grueling process fun and efficient.

INTRODUCTION

My brother-in-law Steve should be a fishing guide. He lives in East Texas and has spent most of his free time fishing for as long as I've known him. He knows every creek, river, and lake in the area. He always knows the best times of the day, the best time of year, and the best type of bait to catch a ton of fish. I have a blast every time I am lucky enough to go fishing with him.

One spring, he invited me out to go fishing for "sandies" on the Sabine River. Some of Steve's friends also brought their boats and came along. Little did I know, on this day I would learn some important rules about fishing and marketing.

Steve and I took off upriver in his boat, and his friends were in their boats. He knew just where to go. After about 20 minutes, we arrived at a spot on the river that looked like an hourglass, where water was rushing through a narrow area and spilling into a wider and calmer section. After Steve showed me the right lure and helped me get my pole rigged for the occasion, we all started fishing. He was catching fish left and right. His friends and I were not having the same luck. Steve looked at me and said, "You're reeling too fast. Slow down." When I began to match his cadence and tempo something amazing happened: I started catching fish!

That day I caught more fish than I ever had before. So much so, I brought enough back to feed my entire family and put several gallon-size freezer bags full of sand bass fillets in the freezer. His friends caught a few fish but not nearly as many as I did, even though they were fishing in the same spot. I had learned the first rule. You can want to catch fish, follow others to the right fishing hole, and even cast in the same spot, but without a guide, someone telling where, what, and how, you won't come home with as many fish as you could have.

Another important rule that came from this adventure was to be consistent and patient and to not give up. Working smart, knowing what to do and how to do it, then putting forth the effort will pay off. It's just difficult to know exactly when that will happen. Those two rules are why I wrote this book. While I don't know much about catching fish, I have spent a lifetime in the Internet waters and I want to be your guide and give you the where, what and how for navigating social media.

Do you remember when the word "Internet" first came into your life? For many people, it was hard to comprehend what the Internet would become and how much it would change our lives. I've been drawn to it even before it was called the Internet. My first exposure came when my dad brought home a CRT terminal and a modem from his office back in the early 1980s. He was in the mainframe outsourcing business, and CRTs and modems were how people connected to those big computers, and the Internet was the way we connected remotely. Back then it was called the ARPANET and you didn't use browsers, there were no graphics and certainly no search engines like Google. I discovered a world of interesting information in the form of Bulletin Board Systems, which were the great-grandfather to blogs, and text-based scenario games that placed you in a game setting and let you choose your next step by answering the question "what's your next move?"

By the early '90s, I was selling the systems that made computers communicate and function to Fortune 100 companies. Back then none of us knew how big this thing called the Internet was going to become. If you had a bricks-and-mortar store, you might not have even bothered to learn about it; perhaps you thought it was something of a fad or it would not affect the way you did business. Oh, how things have changed!

As you have probably guessed, I was part of the Internet bubble and cut my teeth in the modern-day Internet space working for a venture-backed e-commerce company in the late '90s. We were connecting sophisticated shopping carts to the websites of companies who wanted to sell and deliver digital goods such as software and music.

What fascinated me then was how focused the world seemed to be on the transaction side of the Internet but paid little or no attention to marketing. You may remember the UPS television commercial where an e-commerce team had just launched their shopping cart and they were anxiously waiting and watching a sales counter as it sat at zero. Then the first sale happened, which prompted celebratory cheers among the team; then came a few more sales, followed by more cheers. The next thing we saw was the counter moving so fast that you couldn't even recognize the numbers but you could empathize with the frightened looks on the e-commerce team's faces. Now what?

During that time, most of the world had the belief that if you built it they would come; that slapping a shopping cart on a website was all it took to be successful. But that wasn't enough. If the Internet were the alphabet, it seemed to me that the rest of the world was focused on XYZ, which was making a sale and collecting money. No one appeared to be focused on the ABCs—attracting people to their web presence or store and getting them excited about what they had to offer. This was a huge mistake and a big reason why many of the early attempts in the Internet space failed.

To gain value from the Internet requires focus, strategy and effort. As your guide, I want to help you avoid making the same mistakes I have seen so many companies make with regards to social media. They believe that simply having a Facebook page built, starting a blog or making a few videos and putting them up on YouTube is all that's required to succeed in social media. You can't just put your line in the water and expect to catch fish. It's simply not the case. If you're going to succeed, you'll need to follow these steps.

- Develop a game plan that begins with the end in mind for your business as a whole and for each of the social media channels you decide to fish in, such as Twitter, Facebook, LinkedIn, etc.

- Learn the skills for building relationships online with customers, prospects and influencers.

- Understand how to lead with value and create remarkable content that educates and informs.

- Provide reasons for potential customers to want to engage with your company at a deeper level.

Once I saw the need for businesses to apply typical business methods to Internet marketing, I started my own company, WebDex Media Group, to guide business owners through these waters and help their businesses maximize the value that the Internet could play within their organization. In 2008, I began to talk with Splash Media about partnering to deliver video solutions for businesses to tell their story in the medium that was becoming more preferred than text. Two years later, we decided to merge our companies because we saw where the Internet— and specifically social media—was heading and that businesses were going to need a company that could educate, guide, promote, and tell their stories online. Since the merger, we have become the largest social media outsourced provider for small and medium-size companies in the United States.

This gives me a unique perspective to teach you the rules that will help guide you through the social media waters. As a business owner I understand the need to get to the heart of the matter quickly and then connect the dots between social media tactics and real business value. I am also keenly aware that your responsibilities and focus should not be as a practitioner of this social media marketing process; but rather the overseer. As a business owner you don't need to learn the step-by-step method of setting up these systems, but you should be aware of all the available strategies and how to maximize them for your business.

I've also had the opportunity to be a public speaker on the topic of Internet marketing and social media for more than a decade. One thing I've discovered is there are plenty of smart, geeky folks out there who know a lot more about the inner workings of algorithms, source codes and technical Internet programming than I do, but they just don't get the business side of things. I've always tried to think like a business owner and deliver principles and tactics that produce value rather than try to teach people how something is made.

I've been delivering Social Media for CEOs Boot Camps (http://www.splashmedia.com/events/social-media-boot-camp/) on behalf of Splash Media since July 2010, and have trained more than 20,000 business leaders on social media. Our 90-minute boot camp lays the foundation to help companies see the need, and points them in the right direction. The content in this book is a great companion to that event, but even if you haven't attended one of our boot camps I am confident these strategies will help you move your business into the world of social media marketing.

Why this book? There are plenty of books about social media marketing on the bookstore shelves; what makes this one different is that I cut out the BS and I get down to business basics that can only come from hands-on business successes. Since 1998, I've had the opportunity to work with thousands of businesses, from business-to-business, business-to-consumer and industrial to commercial and retail. The rules are the same. If you apply the ones outlined in this book you will succeed.

As you read this book, you will discover the answers to these questions:

- How does social media relate directly to my business marketing?
- How does social media marketing differ from the way I used to advertise?
- Why is it so important from the consumer perspective?
- What makes social media marketing a revolution?
- Why will traditional marketing continue to erode, and how can I effectively shift my advertising budget?
- What are the best practices in social media and how can I use them effectively?
- Why will the messages used in traditional marketing no longer work?
- Why should I consider myself a micropublisher?
- Why is social media marketing synonymous with Search Engine Optimization 2.0?

- What is 'reputation management' in social media?
- What are the best strategies for getting started?

Social Rules! will provide you with strategic dos and don'ts and help you determine how to implement the best tools. Whether you do this in-house by utilizing a current employee or hire a consultant to help you accomplish these goals, you'll learn the optimal rules of engagement and how to measure results.

I will introduce and guide you through the *Tactical Wheel of Social Media Marketing*. This is a specific method of maximizing your efforts for each and every social media platform. It begins with Listening, which is a specific way to watch what is happening online and identify influencers and potential customers so you can easily move into engagement and create your community. I will explain the importance of *Building Community* and show you how to motivate your community of current customers, prospects and employees to engage with you so you begin seeing progress for your business. Next, you'll learn about *Broadcasting* and how to post social media content in such a way as to draw people into your environment and why that's so important. I will explain how to develop compelling social media *Content* so you are always adding value. You'll learn how to use your content and messaging appropriately for *Conversion* by encouraging people to talk to a salesperson or engage with your company at a deeper level.

There's a plethora of social media platforms coming on the scene every single day and some of them will be here today and gone tomorrow. We'll focus on what we call the foundational sites: Facebook, Twitter, LinkedIn, YouTube and your blog. If you focus your energies on these primary platforms and really pay attention to the activity and engagement taking place within them, you'll be in excellent position to optimize social media marketing.

Some people fear change and others embrace it, but regardless of our approach, change is inevitable. I am excited that you have picked up this book and chosen me to be your guide as you embark on a journey into this new and exciting era of marketing. You may not have as much fun reading my book as I did that day fishing on the Sabine River; however, if you follow the practical steps outlined in these pages, I believe that you'll find and acquire new customers and build strong and lasting relationships that benefit your business greatly.

Part 1

NEW RULES OF MARKETING

1. THE RULES HAVE CHANGED

You might be part of the group of business owners who initially dismissed social media marketing. Perhaps you believed the people playing in that arena were not your target market. You may have even felt too comfortable in your traditional ways to consider embracing what might be a fad. If you have previously dug your heels in and resisted this change, don't worry—I will ease you into it. But first we need to take a true look at exactly what is happening and how it can help us move forward.

Traditional advertising and the way companies have gone to market for the past two hundred years is going to continue to be an acceptable way to sell products and to get people excited about what companies provide. But it can no longer stand on its own. What has been effective in the past is not as effective today. As companies spend more money to make less, it is only natural that a shift has to occur.

Since the mid-1990s, the evolution of Internet marketing has been a major contributor to the way we communicate who we are as businesses, what services and products we have available, and the way we engage with consumers. Some people might think social media is just an extension of Internet marketing because it takes place on the Internet. They might see it as an evolution of what has been happening over the years. I really don't believe social media is an evolution, and if you treat it as one, what's really happening might pass you by.

Social media is, in and of itself, a *revolution*. It models the characteristics of a revolution because there has been a sudden and marked change in the rules of engagement as well a shift in power. Within a revolution there is typically a shift from a limited few having the power over many to the masses taking the reins. That's one of the biggest reasons why I would call social media a revolution more than an evolution—the power has shifted from big media and big businesses to the people. In a very short time there has been a huge shift in enabling the average person or consumer to be a contributor to the conversation as well as a change agent.

This shift has made all of us micropublishers: the amount of web content we're creating as consumers or individuals today far exceeds anything corporations are able to communicate. This has created what I call "content competition." Traditional advertising was more effective in the '90s because there was a limited amount of content and a huge percentage of it was owned by companies wanting to get their message out to the masses. Today the sea of content is much broader, and a huge percentage of that content is published by individuals sharing their thoughts and opinions and reviews related to their experiences.

It's also extremely fragmented now. If you think back to the late 1990s, there were limited channels from which consumers could get information; today those channels are infinite. In fact, at the time of this writing, there are more than 100 million blogs on the web, which is equivalent to the number of active commercial websites here in the United States. That number doesn't even include what is happening on Twitter and Facebook. On Twitter there are more than 140 million tweets posted every single day of the week, which is up from 50 million just a year ago. On Facebook there are over 700 million active users, and 70 % of Internet users in the United States have a profile on Facebook today, with the average user publishing 90 pieces of content a month. Do the math and you'll find that's 45 billion pieces of content each month.

That is why I call this a revolution. The power has shifted to the people and it has happened very rapidly. This change has led to word-of-mouth advertising at its most extreme. In the past we would often make buying decisions based on what our close friends had to say about a product or service. Now we make these same decisions based on input from people we have never met and who we trust more than what a brand or company would say about their products.

Another key factor in the weakening of traditional advertising is that we have become a content-on-demand society. As consumers we've learned that the price for quality content is no longer advertising; instead we can get the content from a company or online resource whenever we want it and however we want it. If we want to watch a television show, we don't have to be sitting in front of the TV at a certain time of day. Instead we can watch it on our iPad, iPhone, computer, or our television whenever we want and with the luxury of fast-forwarding through the commercials. In fact, 90 % of people who have TiVos or DVRs at home today are fast-forwarding through the commercials because we no longer tolerate "interruption advertising." This type of advertising was a primary method of traditional marketing in which companies relied on their ability to catch us doing something we enjoyed and interrupt us with a marketing message. We can now take control of these messages by using TV devices, satellite and Internet radio stations, and powerful spam filters on our email accounts. To combat the consumer's control over when, where, and how advertisements were seen, traditional media decided to bombard us with even more messages. This concept of simply turning up the dial resulted in the average US consumer being blasted with 3,000 advertising messages every single day.

Consumers Rebel

Revolutions typically start with a rebellion, and what we're seeing today is that social media has given consumers a voice and a weapon to speak out against interruption advertising, such as TV commercials, spam, etc. We're also rebelling against half-truth advertising messages and slick marketing techniques. Regardless of whether or not you are a fan of reality TV, you can recognize the popularity of reality-based shows as a rebellion against the more contrived and often slick television shows like ER or Law and Order We want to see realism today, and we want real information and to be told the truth. Because we have a new voice within social media, we're rebelling against poor service, poor quality, and the misrepresentation of facts.

For example, my family loves to go to the beach on vacation, and typically we try to go at least every couple of years. I rely on the Internet to help us find a place to stay, whether we're going to Florida or California. Through the years I've had good and bad experiences looking on the Internet for pictures of a condo or a hotel and the nearby beaches. On occasion I have been extremely disappointed in the discrepancy between the photos posted and the reality once we arrived. Now I don't book anything until I go online and check out Trip Advisor—a social site where people post comments about their experiences with the accommodations they've used. Once I narrow down a few options I search on Trip Advisor to see what other people have to say about the locations. Then I make my final decision based on their comments. Once again, the power has truly shifted from companies posting slick pictures of their hotel or condo to being able to read feedback from people who have already stayed there. I love making a more informed decision and avoiding the disappointment of bringing my family to a place they won't enjoy.

The Revolutions That Paved the Way for Social Media

Social media isn't the first revolution in the world of digital or electronic media. Radio, television, and the Internet each had a sudden impact on the way individuals consumed information and the way businesses reached their customers. The radio was a huge revolution because prior to its introduction there was no way to deliver content simultaneously across the entire country. If you weren't in an urban area, you shopped using the Sears catalog that arrived in the mail. This is how you discovered things you wanted to purchase. But when radio became widely available, people were able to gain instant access to content, and advertisers had an easy and effective way to get their message to the masses. Even if you weren't around to hear the broadcast, you're probably familiar with the famous Orson Welles *War of the Worlds* radio broadcast in 1938 that created a panic across the entire United States. Prior to the radio, that kind of nationwide impact wouldn't have been possible.

Television added pictures to what was happening in the world of radio, and it was also a revolution because it impacted our perception and the way we interpreted information and made decisions. A perfect example is the 1960 debate between presidential candidates Richard M. Nixon and John F. Kennedy. It was the first nationally televised debate, and Nixon refused to wear makeup while Kennedy not only wore makeup but he was also younger and had a better television presence. Kennedy came across more likable on television and ended up winning the election. However, when people who only listened to the debate on the radio were polled, they overwhelmingly believed Nixon won the debate.

The big impact the Internet had over television or radio was instant access to information and the ability for consumers to purchase items twenty-four hours a day, seven days a week. For instance, if you want to learn how to fly fish, you can get on the Internet and within ten minutes you'll have a good rudimentary understanding of what it's all about. If you want to learn more you can go to Amazon.com and buy a book any time of the day or night.

SOCIAL MEDIA FACTS & STATS

- The radio took 38 years to reach 50 million users.
- The television took 13 years to reach 50 million users.
- The Internet took 4 years to reach 50 million users.
- Facebook added 200 million users in 2010 alone (now that's a revolution!).
- 50% of the world's population is younger than the age of 30.
- 96% of the millennial generation in the United States are using social media. (If we just think about the impact that the baby boomers have had on our society, we have to realize the millennial generation are going to be a bigger part of our society than the baby boomers very soon.)
- 80% of US companies are using social media to recruit new employees.
- 24 of the 25 largest newspapers are experiencing record declines because we're a content-on-demand society.
- 90% of people with TVs and DVRs skip ads on television.
- 73% of active online users have read blogs.

See the appendix for sources of the stats provided above.

As you can see by these statistics, social media is a bigger revolution than even radio, TV, and the Internet because it has truly put the power in the hands of the people. A colleague of mine is a great example of this power shift. He and his girlfriend competed in the Warrior Dash, an intense obstacle-course race held all over the country. It's an endurance race that spans only a few miles, but the competitors must run through mud, up extreme inclines, and navigate military-type obstacles. It is not for the weak. Like many sponsored races, there were photographers set up throughout the course taking pictures that were posted on the Internet and available for purchase. My colleague wanted to buy a few pictures but was outraged that they were selling for eighty dollars each for downloaded photos that would still need to be printed. The price didn't even include shipping costs. He decided to go on Facebook and find the company that was taking the pictures on behalf of the Warrior Dash, and he posted a comment on their wall about how he thought that was an unfair price. In a very short time, hundreds of people joined in the conversation and agreed the price was outrageous. The next day the company published its own wall post offering to sell the photos at half price to anyone who participated in the Warrior Dash. That type of savings would have never happened on that large of a scale prior to social media.

Not All Revolutions Are Alike

Think about the last time you landed on a piece of content on the Internet, such as a website, blog, or video. Did you read the entire thing? Did you watch the entire video, or did you see it was five minutes long and decided to cut it short? My guess is you hardly ever go through online content in its entirety. We are bombarded with so much content today that we can't afford to pay attention to everything that comes into our lives. It's almost as if we've given ourselves attention deficient disorder, and in our rush to get the best information in the shortest amount of time we are using other people to help us curate what content is important. This has put pressure on the old-school marketing strategies that use a shotgun approach to reach their target markets, which really creates collateral damage for both the advertiser and the consumer. The damage to the marketer is wasted advertising dollars, and the damage to the consumer is dealing with useless information they really aren't interested in anyway. Traditional marketing has always been forced to deal with waste that consists of dollars spent getting a marketing message in front of people who have no interest in what is being sold. This approach creates even more waste because traditional advertising is sold by demographic and reach, with little regard to interest.

For instance, if you were trying to reach a teenage female target, you might advertise your shampoo product using commercials that air during *American Idol*. You'd spend a lot of money for an ad that was being seen by millions of people who did not fit your demographic and who probably got up from the couch or fast-forwarded right through it. The difference between your TV ad and social media marketing is with social media marketing you are not competing for attention because it exists within a buyer-initiated media. The advertiser is no longer the one taking the first step to educate the consumer. Instead it's the consumer who is initiating their own education and gaining the information and knowledge they need to make an informed buying decision.

I live in a suburb of Dallas called Flower Mound, which is a relatively new area that didn't exist when I first left Dallas in the early 1990s to go to St. Louis. When I came back I moved into Flower Mound because it was a nice area and it was close to the airport. Because it's a transient area and a lot of people were coming in from other states and cities, the typical house would flip owners about every five years. This constant real estate activity led to me receiving new postcards in the mail literally every single day from real estate agents asking me if I wanted to sell or buy a new home. I receive that postcard because I fulfill one filter on their demographic criteria: I'm a homeowner in Flower Mound. Unfortunately they are wasting their marketing collateral on me because they don't know anything else about me as an individual. They don't know I have an eleven-year-old daughter in the sixth grade, and I have no intention of selling my house until she graduates from high school seven years from now. Needless to say, the postcards go right from the mailbox to the trash. In the world of social media there is no waste because by default you are connecting with an interested audience. Your audience is opting-in to your business by joining you in the online conversation.

A Shift in Content

Because of this revolution, only 14 % of consumers really believe company advertising messages are true anymore, and this is a significant shift over the last four to five years (Social Marketing Industry Report, 2010). Consumer confidence based on our marketing messages is dwindling; conversely, 78 % of consumers will believe what a complete stranger says about a company's products or services. Because the rules have changed, a complete stranger now has more influence over a buying decision than a company's traditional marketing message.

The cause of this is individuals are shifting from consumers of content to creators of content. We're giving feedback through social media on a great dinner or a bad one at a specific restaurant. We're recommending to colleagues and friends products we've enjoyed and those we would never waste money on again. We're complaining on blogs about slow or poor service for anyone to read.

Based on everything I've discussed so far, we're not going to be able to turn off the spigot. Consumers will not suddenly stop using social media. It will continue to permeate our society, and people will leverage the power that social media has given them to communicate to their friends—and to companies—their likes, dislikes, and opinions related to products or services.

Change always equals opportunity. However, whenever there's a shift, there's always resistance to change. That resistance creates opportunity for those who are willing to embrace the change. Don't be fearful of this shift; embrace it and become excited about the fact that it's a revolution, and as a business owner you can participate in it rather than be a victim of it.

Two Fundamental Rules

There are two foundational rules that many of the premises of this book are built upon, and these rules will not change even though we're in the midst of a revolution. *The first is, people do business with people.* We will always do business with people we feel connected to and trust. The second is, *people love to buy and they hate to be sold.* As a business leader, you can help people buy rather than sell to them by letting your personality and company culture shine through social media.

Think about how you can influence consumers more than merely sell your product. What can you do to get people talking about you rather than only *you* talking about you? You need to lead with value and educate your target audience to help them make their lives better. We want to empower your customers to become evangelists for your business through social media. If you're a business that has been around for a while, you no doubt have happy customers, and those happy customers have friends and followers who are interested in what they have to say about your products or services. Empower them by giving them a voice.

As you venture into social media, you will need to understand that it is a two-way conversation requiring listening and participating more than just talking. You can no longer vie for attention by interrupting your customers; you have to participate in their communities and in their conversations. You also can't wait for them to come to you. You have to go to them. Just don't forget that it's *their* conversation, and you are just participating.

2. WHAT IS SOCIAL MEDIA MARKETING?

Social media marketing is the process of delivering value to the consumer in online communities where they congregate. By delivering value via social media channels, potential customers will:

1. Become aware of your business,
2. Begin to build trust in your company,
3. Begin to share your information with their peers,
4. Ultimately begin to purchase products and services from you.

The key point to all of this is delivering value to consumers where they congregate. It's not about interrupting them or yelling at them to get their attention, as has often been the case with traditional marketing. It's no longer about them coming to you. It's about you delivering value where they are.

Another key point to understand about social media marketing is that it's a two-way conversation where the consumer is an active participant. That's a big difference from the world of traditional marketing, which is a monologue consisting of you asking someone to buy from you and walking away before you even give them a chance to say "yes" or "no." Social media marketing is about building a relationship through conversation with your target audience. In many cases the customer starts the dialogue and you are jumping in and participating in their conversation.

Because so much of it is about dialogue, social media marketing success is dependent on effective communication skills. It's as much about communicating as it is about marketing. Skills such as acknowledging thoughts and opinions, offering advice, providing encouragement, and responding to questions are the tenets of an effective social media marketing campaign. In many ways social media marketing is the inside out and upside down marketing process. You almost need to take everything you've thought in the past about the way to get your marketing message out to your targeted audience and throw it out the window.

It's like operating in the inverse of what you've always done before.

- The old value-add has been replaced by leading with value. It's about giving away something of value to your customer first and not waiting until they buy something from you before you deliver value.

- Rather than interrupting, you are now responding. In the world of social media you should respond to conversations and not interrupt them with your marketing message like a traditional radio commercial or a television commercial.

- Instead of a monologue, communication is now a dialogue.

- The company is no longer in control of the conversation; the customer is.

- Barraging the customer to get their attention like a snake oil salesman has shifted to the role of a camp counselor providing advice.

Social media marketing is the antithesis of what might have worked in the past. The world is changing and a revolution is occurring and people are expecting companies to behave differently as a result of this revolution.

To expand on Seth Godin's insights in his book, *Permission Marketing*, social media marketing is a process of turning strangers into friends, friends into customers, and customers into evangelists. It's like courtship. If I had asked my now wife of 20-plus years to marry me the first time I approached her, she would have thought I was crazy and I would have missed the opportunity to develop a relationship and start a family with her. Just like in courtship, the first thing you need to do in social media marketing is spend a little time together with your existing customers and potential customers. Start out with dating and over time build a relationship and then eventually you can move from courtship into marriage.

Social media marketing has stages, just like dating, courtship and marriage. Once you gain customers through social media, they will be stuck to you like glue. Let's break down the stages.

Turning strangers into friends: This is done by searching for them and participating in social media conversations that are happening between customers, potential customers, competitors, and partners. It is perfectly okay to engage in a conversation with a competitor or an influencer because your potential customers are able to see those conversations in the public domain.

Turning friends into customers: This is accomplished by leading with value, answering questions, and waiting patiently to help people or companies improve their situation with your products or services. Remember you have something of value to offer or you would not be in business. Ultimately you need to get out of the mindset that you have something to sell and switch to finding a way to help an individual or a company achieve an objective by leveraging your product or service.

Turning customers into evangelists: The best way to make this happen is to deliver a good product or service coupled with amazing customer service. Notice that I said a good product and amazing customer service. This is an interesting component of social media. Your product doesn't have to be amazing. At the end of the day that depends on what price you are offering, who are the customers you are trying to reach, and what value you produce. Whether or not you have a good product or an amazing product, you must be able to deliver amazing customer service. That's a key part of social media marketing and turning customers into evangelists.

You then need to provide platforms for your customers to share their stories about how much they love your company and love your service. These platforms would be your various social media accounts. Simply stated, this is word-of-mouth advertising on steroids.

Tried and True Lessons

In preparing to write this book, I took myself through a little refresher course by taking out my well-worn copy of Dale Carnegie's, *How to Win Friends and Influence People* written in 1936. As I was rereading the book, I was blown away with how something written in the middle of the Great Depression remains relevant today, especially when it comes to social media marketing.

I want to review just a few key points Dale Carnegie highlights in his book (It is time well spent.)

- Don't criticize, condemn, or complain. You are certainly not going to do this in social media marketing for the whole world to see.

- Give honest and sincere appreciation.

- Become genuinely interested in other people. It's when you are interested in them that they become interested in you.

- A person's name is the sweetest and most important sound to them, in any language. Referencing their name and engaging and communicating with them will do you well in social media.

- Be a good listener. Later in the book there is an entire chapter dedicated to listening and how to do if effectively in social media marketing.

- Encourage others to talk about themself.

- Talk in terms of the other person's interest.

- Make the other person feel important and do it sincerely.

- Show respect for the other person's opinions and never say they are wrong.

- If you are wrong, admit it quickly and emphatically.

- Be sympathetic with the other person's ideas and desires.

- Begin with praise and honest appreciation.

Social Media Marketing from Consumer Perspective

Social media marketing is important to the consumer because we are quickly becoming a content-on-demand society. Customers have the power to consume any type of content, in any form or fashion, from anywhere. Whether it's on our phone, laptop, iPad, sitting in front of the television or at a sporting event, we can receive any type of content we want, whenever we want it. As a result, most people are tuning out commercials. Instead of relying on advertising, we're using the web extensively to research information about products and services we want to buy and about ways to solve problems and improve our lives. We are also spending a lot of time on social sites, engaging with Facebook, and LinkedIn, and Twitter to gather this information.

In fact, we are also spending more time online than ever before. According to a Forrester Research Study from December 2010, Americans are spending as much time on the Internet as they do watching TV, with Internet usage soaring 121% over the previous five years. Additionally, a Pew research study from August 2010 cited these interesting facts regarding social media usage:

- Nearly 50% of 50-64 year-olds are now active on social media!
- 86% of Americans between the ages of 18-29 are active in social media.
- 61% of the 30-49 crowd are active online.

By the chart below, you can see these segments are growing substantially year over year.

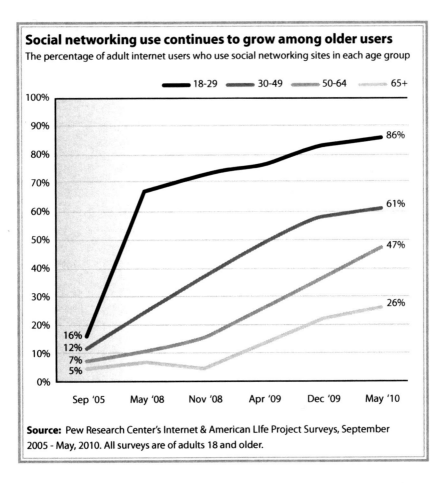

What do you think it's going to look like ten years from now?

Innovation doesn't care about us. It will leave us in the dust if we don't grab hold. My guess is there were some really great candle companies around at the time Edison was inventing the light bulb, and they had no choice: adapt or be left in the dark. When innovation strikes, it's almost impossible to go back to the way things were. However, the fuel to innovation is always the value it provides to the masses. We would all agree that having things like the light bulb and electricity are good for society.

The best way to grab hold of social media is to remember your company's purpose and the value you provide customers, then find a way to achieve that purpose in this new media. The newspaper industry failed because they forgot they were in the information business and began to falsely believe they were in the printing business. Travel agents failed because they thought they were in the business of selling seats on airplanes and rooms in hotels, and forgot that they were really in the business of selling convenience to business people and lifelong memories to vacationing families.

A great case study in adapting with innovation is IBM. IBM has roots back to the late 1880s. Since that time IBM has reinvented itself over and over to continue to deliver value to their customers in an ever-changing world, from accounting machines to computers to software and finally to services. Their Global Services division accounts for 57% of their revenue today. I have been fascinated by IBM since the early '90s and over the years have seen them embrace the Internet and now social media with gusto. They aren't afraid of change; they embrace it! As a happy shareholder in the company, I have also seen their stock price double during the last decade while other companies' stock prices have taken a real beating.

View social media marketing as an opportunity for your business to fulfill its purpose in ways you have never imagined. Don't hold onto things that will prevent you from embracing it. This might mean reevaluating how you spend your marketing dollars or developing a new marketing strategy altogether. Don't head down the road of travel agents and the newspaper industry, but rather become nimble and adapt and you will find plenty of new opportunities within social media.

3. ADDITIONAL BENEFITS TO SOCIAL MEDIA

So far we've touched on how to leverage social media to turn strangers into friends, friends into customers and customers into evangelists. Now it's time to help you see the other important benefits and components of social media that are important to your business.

Reputation Management

Reputation management is managing what is being said online, primarily within social sites, about your company or the products and services that you provide. It's important to understand that there are conversations going on in social media and the web about your industry, company, products and services, regardless of whether your company is active in the online communities. Let's also dispel the myth that by having a presence and being active in social media you are exposing yourself and inviting negative comments from your customers. I hear that a lot at the social media boot camps I present. People come up to me and say they don't want to get into social media marketing because they fear that as soon as they set up a Facebook page, Twitter account or a blog, customers will use those platforms to publically complain about their company. My response to them is the same as it is to you. *Positive and negative conversations are already happening, so why not make sure you know where they are so you can address them quickly and effectively?*

One value you'll receive by getting in the game is you're

creating an opportunity for those conversations to happen in an environment where you can react immediately and take control. Don't think that just because you are getting into social media is *the reason* why you are going to have to deal with reputation management. It's just the smart and proactive response to what's already happening in the world today.

The goal for reputation management is respond first, then repair or reward. You will see throughout this chapter that reputation management isn't just about dealing with negative issues and feedback regarding your brand. It's also about having a strategy to maximize the positive reactions and make sure those people are being rewarded. These are the evangelists I alluded to earlier; leveraging evangelists is the Holy Grail when it comes to social media marketing.

Social media provides tremendous opportunities to showcase to your customers that you are listening and you care. A client of mine said there are two times during the life of a customer that you can prove you are worth the investment they made in you. One is at the time of the sale, when you made a compelling argument for them to say yes. The second time you can prove your worth is when there is a problem. Rather than see problems as bad things embrace them as opportunities to demonstrate to your customer how much you truly care about them and their business, and that you want to make things right. Reputation management should be seen from the perspective of these two valuable opportunities to turn your customers into evangelists.

Reputation management starts with listening. The best way to listen is to be aware, and notified, of every time your brand and variation of your company name is being mentioned online. For example, the name of my company is Splash Media, so I listen for any mention of Splash Media as two words or SplashMedia as one word, just Splash and even Splash Social Media. Make sure you are listening for the name of your products and services as well. There is an entire chapter in this book dedicated to listening, but for now I wanted to briefly mention that one way to set up an effective and efficient listening system is to use Google Alerts for daily notifications of your company name, products and services being mentioned in blogs, articles, etc.

Manage your reputation by having an active community manager. This is another key part to making reputation management work. Your community manager can be you or it can be somebody in your organization. Your community manager should be a real-time social media customer service person. This is the person who will be monitoring conversations and when something positive or negative is said about your company, this community manager should be able to see it and react quickly.

As I've mentioned before, we are becoming a content-on-demand society and customers are beginning to expect companies to respond when they make comments about their experiences. They also expect your response even if they don't make a comment directly on your Facebook wall, but they mention you on Twitter or in some other social media environment.

For example, last fall my wife and I went on a trip to the British Virgin Isles to celebrate our 20th wedding anniversary. On the way to our destination, the major airline we chose lost a piece of luggage and it took two days for us to get it back. Then, on our return trip we had to change planes in Miami. Our plane sat on the tarmac for 45 minutes as we squirmed in our seats, worried about the possibility of missing our connecting flight. We finally were able to exit the plane 10 minutes before our next flight was scheduled to leave for Dallas. When we got to the gate, we could see our plane sitting next to the gate, but the entrance to the walkway was locked down and the staff rudely told us that our flight, the last flight to Dallas that day, was closed—we had missed the "final boarding call." It turned out that while we, the handful of people who were on the first flight, were having a lively discussion with the gate agent; the pilot had a clear view of our exchange. Seeing us beg the agent to let us on the plane prompted the pilot to take mercy on us and he instructed the agent to let us board.

I had cashed in all of my frequent flyer miles so that we could fly in first class on the way home, but because of the delay, the airline had given away our seats. Not only did we not get to enjoy the comfort of first class, my wife and I did not even get to sit near each other. She was at the front of the plane and I was stuck in a middle seat further back for the entire flight. That was not how I wanted to end our anniversary celebration and I was certainly not pleased with wasting all of those miles for the upgrade.

While I was sitting on the tarmac in Miami, and as soon as we landed and headed for the gate in Dallas, I was berating the airline on Twitter with a hashtag and their company name because I was so unhappy with them. I think the hashtag #Fail was used more than once also. For me, it wasn't just about complaining to anyone who would listen; I was expecting someone from the company to reach out to me and at least apologize. I was surprised and disappointed that I never heard from anyone and it will definitely affect my buying decision in the future. The airline's lack of response may have a lot to do with not having a community manager or established policies for responding to online comments. Unfortunately it is affecting their business and they may not even know it.

Imagine what would have happened if someone from the airline had responded and apologized for my issues, maybe even worked with their frequent flyer department to ensure that my miles were credited back and then some. If that had happened, I might even have used them as a successful case study in my book and mentioned them by name. Instead they will remain the nameless airline who tried to ruin my anniversary and who I try to avoid flying with at all costs.

I guess I'm not the only one frustrated with this airline. Notice that there are NO responses from the airline. I guess they are not listening to their customers.

Maximizing Good Comments

What should you do when good things are said about your company online, either through social media sites or on your website? The first thing you want to do is thank them for their comments and then reward them publicly. I am not recommending that every positive comment earns a reward; however, I do encourage you to come up with something you can give away to people who praise you online. Try to give something away about every third or fourth time a person shares something positive. It could be as simple as a coupon for a discount or even a free meal the next time they come to your restaurant. The result will be that you'll start training the people watching you (followers, likes/fans) to engage in a conversation and also share positive comments about your business.

Another thing you want to do with the positive comments is ask the person an open-ended question to keep the good conversation going. For instance, if someone shared about having a great time at an educational event you hosted and they learned a lot, you might thank them for attending and ask them to tell you about their favorite part. Or, if they talk about how great your product is, you can ask them what type of results they received and encourage them to share it with you publicly.

If you see a positive comment shared via Twitter, you should definitely re-tweet the entire status update and share it with your followers. Also reply back to that person publicly and ask an open-ended question to keep the dialogue going. You want to give your evangelists every opportunity to toot your horn as long as possible and to reward them with public recognition and a perhaps a reward.

Handling Negative Comments

As the world becomes more social and people have more access to social environments on the fly through mobile devices, negative comments in the heat of the moment will be inevitable. You need to be prepared in advance for a company-wide, acceptable response policy that can also be flexible on a case-by-case basis.

The very first thing to do when bad comments occur is to immediately thank the customers for bringing it to your attention. No matter how it makes you feel, you have to be extremely gracious and appreciative of their efforts to alert you of their situation. Do this publicly so your followers see how professional and prompt you are at handling issues. Next, publicly offer to resolve the issue, but ask if you can do it offline by giving them the opportunity to direct message you and share more details regarding their experience and concern. Offer your direct phone number and invite them to call you or come to your location.

The goal is to acknowledge publicly and resolve privately. Once the conversation goes offline there are two things that you want to determine: do they have a valid complaint, or did they misinterpret your offering and have unrealistic expectations?

They have a valid complaint. If it's a valid complaint you should fix it and then give them something for their trouble. For example, if the customers had a bad meal at your restaurant, invite them back for a free dinner for up to five people. Perhaps they were poorly treated by your customer service department; so you offer them their next month's service for free. If they had a long delay in receiving their order, send them a gift card valued at 50% off their next purchase.

They misunderstood the offer or had unrealistic expectations.

Proper communication about the product and setting realistic expectations is *your* responsibility and not the responsibility of the customer. Even if your customers misunderstood the offer and have unrealistic expectations, it's your problem and not theirs because you didn't sell your product or service appropriately. First, apologize for not properly communicating what the product or service would do and then offer to upgrade the service or allow them to return the product.

For example, let's say they purchased nutritional supplements to lose weight and they actually gained weight because they didn't use the product properly. You need to remind them that in order for your product to work it has to be combined with exercise or a reduction of their caloric intake. Also, send them a free bottle or refund their money.

Another example is when a customer brings a coupon to your store and it's not eligible for the discount. Perhaps they already bought the product a few days ago and then discovered your coupon in the paper and they want a refund for the difference. Your store clerk may have mishandled the request and now they're bringing it to your attention through social media. Apologize for the inconvenience and offer to give them the discount or a 100% refund.

Once you resolve the issue, regardless of whether it is a valid complaint or a misunderstanding, encourage the customer to go back online and comment about their experience. The goal is to have them say something about how well you bent over backwards to fix a problem, which shows their followers how much you care about your customers.

If you can take 100% of the complaints online and deal with

them the way I have outlined, you might get 20% of them to go back and say something positive about you. You have now turned unhappy customers into evangelists.

At the beginning of this book, remember I mentioned that to succeed in social media you can have a good product, but you have to have amazing customer service? This is how you deliver amazing customer service through social media.

Detecting fake negative comments. You might discover that some of the negative comments being made about your brand are coming from a competitor who is trying to sabotage your business. I call this social media terrorism, but these individuals are usually referred to as trolls. We've had this happen at Splash Media and to some of our customers. Just like dealing with negative comments, you should have a strategy for how to handle this when it happens.

There are two conditions in which a troll or social media terrorism might occur. One could be inside an environment, like Facebook, that you can control by monitoring and deleting the comments and letting the platform know what is happening. For example, we had a competitor come onto our Facebook page under a fake profile and stir up negativity about our company. We were able to validate that the profile wasn't a real person and when we brought it to the attention of Facebook, they deleted their profile.

The second condition is on Twitter or Yelp, in which you cannot control the troll's posts. Again, try to validate that it is a competitor and when you can prove it, notify the network provider and ask that the reviews be deleted off your profile.

Customer Service Concierge

In addition to using reputation management to deal with comments customers make about your company, you can also maximize the customer's experience by becoming a customer service concierge. This idea of leading with customer service rather than waiting for your customer to request help will create an environment to turn customers into evangelists.

Think for a moment about when you stay in a hotel for business or pleasure. You rely and expect the concierge to be your go-to person for all your needs and wants. You expect them to always be there, available, smiling and eager to help you. It could be simply to show you where your event is taking place make reservations at a restaurant or find special seating for a show. Their job is to make sure you have a great experience at their hotel and in their city so you become a raving fan and loyal customer.

If you can embrace this concept and become the social media concierge for your industry, your customers will be greatly satisfied and will surely tell others about the terrific service you provide. Again, this is word-of-mouth-advertising on steroids. Don't just think about it from a problem-solving perspective but also from an experience perspective. Concierge services answer questions, provide advice, make connections, connect the dots and make sure your time spent in and even around their environment is pleasurable, and they always do it with a smile on their face.

This concept is a homerun if your customer starts to think of your social media channels this way. I love it when people reach out through social media and ask for help. Recently someone was tweeting about needing some statistics on social media usage. I had just researched that topic for this book, so I replied back with links to the information. He was very appreciative. Did he buy something from me? No. But in the world of social media, you never know who is watching. My hope is I made a good impression and either he'll come back or someone else was paying attention and will use Splash Media's services after seeing multiple examples like that one.

Make Twitter, Facebook and your blog a place customers and prospects can go to experience that level of service. To make this work you'll have to anticipate the questions and needs of your customers so you'll be able to respond quickly. You need to be prepared to deliver value even if that means you won't make a sale. You also need to be actively listening so you can jump in and help your customers move through the process of making a decision about a product or service.

One of my favorite stories about being a social media concierge is told by Gary Vaynerchuk. Gary took his dad's liquor store business from about $4 million in sales to over $50 million by leveraging social media. One of the ways he did this was by listening on Twitter for people talking about going out for dinner. He then jumped in on their conversation and offered to make suggestions on a good wine pairing for their meal. Here's a guy in New York City talking to people all over the world about what wine would go best with their meal. There was no way he could make a sale at that moment. However, by being a social media concierge for his industry, he created so much goodwill that when he started selling wine online, his business exploded. For more details about his success, see the YouTube chapter in this book.

Optimizing Your Social CRM

CRM is an acronym that stands for Customer Relationship Management. As you know, traditional CRM has been around for a long time. In fact CRM has been around as long as we've had customers, but over the last 15-20 years we have thought about CRM from a perspective of using technology to help us manage our customers more effectively. Social media can play a significant role in the way you manage your relationship with customers, but you have to meet them where they are.

What we are seeing now as the result of the social media revolution is customers are expecting you to deliver customer service to them. This means you must be prepared to manage your customer relationships in the different social media platforms where your customers spend time. Customers are getting pretty tired of coming to you via the phone and waiting on hold for 20 minutes or wasting time on your website. In fact, they don't like that idea at all, and they believe you should not expect them to work too hard to get help anymore.

As I mentioned earlier problems are opportunities. We know our customers don't want to be kept on hold or have to repeat their issues as they are transferred to numerous departments. Unfortunately, we have trained our customers that getting good customer service through our traditional channels is a painful thing with a low probability of making them happy. As a result, often what happens is rather than trying to get help they just complain online. Why not meet them where they are and actually deliver good customer service right then and there? This is where your own community management is so absolutely crucial. Your community manager must listen for opportunities to help and encourage users to bring their customer service issues to you via social media. By turning your social media platforms into customer relationship management centers and customer service environments, you can begin to ask your community for suggestions about how to improve your company, and its products and services. Once these types of conversations start occurring, your community will begin to take part in the conversation by answering questions other customers ask. Now all of a sudden you have this unpaid resource that's out there using your product(s) every single day and helping your other customers deal with their issues. Customers helping customers right before your very eyes for the whole world to see is what I call incredible customer relationship management. There is no advertising in the world that can deliver this type of goodwill for your business.

Leverage social media for product development and product improvement

Customers who live with your product every single day can be a great resource of market research and product development. Social media offers an opportunity to improve your company's products or services by tapping into customers:

1. To understand how they are using the product or service

2. To learn from requests or comments what other features you might need to add to your products. Pay attention if people are saying they wish your product or service could do this or they hate when it does that. That's great intelligence about what you can do on future releases or enhancements to your product.

3. You can even use your community for beta testing and gaining feedback. If you have a product you're about to

launch into the market and you want to get good user perspective, your community of followers on social media is a great place to test it.

4. Another part of using social media for product development or product improvement is to listen to your customers talking about your products and services and invite them to join a group or forum about making improvements. It will make for a great group on Facebook or LinkedIn to act as a forum for a community discussion. The whole purpose of that forum is to come up with ideas to enhance and make your product better.

While the majority of this book will offer strategies, tactics and advice on how to use social media to grow sales, we can't forget the other benefits that social media can offer your company. As you read on, you will see how in reality all of the points made in this chapter are really interwoven in the way you will turn strangers into friends, friends into customers and customers into evangelists.

4. SOCIAL MEDIA MARKETING = SEARCH ENGINE OPTIMIZATION 2.0

The Internet world has changed significantly over the past 10-12 years as it relates to search engine optimization. When WebDex launched back in 2000, our initial mission was to generate favorable search engine rankings for our clients. As you can imagine, the most common goal from companies who contacted us about SEO back then was to be ranked No.1 in Yahoo!, AltaVista and Lycos. Times have changed. It's funny to realize that of those three websites, only one is still a serious contender today, and even Yahoo! has lost so much of its favor.

Today, Google is king when it comes to search engine usage. What makes Google's ranking methods superior to the other search engines is the way they understand the relevance between one website and another. It's not about keyword stuffing or only making sure you have keywords in the right place; what's more relevant is what other websites think about your website. We'll get into more of that later.

What is SEO?

Search engine optimization is really the art of effectively communicating to the search engines what each of the individual pieces of content you produce are all about. When I say content, I'm referring to web pages, blogs, video, press releases, and images. Think of SEO as a communication method that operates from a key phrase perspective. Begin with the end in mind and think about the words and phrases your potential customers are typing into sites like Google when they formulate their buying criteria. You need to understand what those words and phrases are in order to create content and build a search engine optimization strategy around making sure you're effectively communicating those relevant topics. There are two components to building a solid SEO strategy.

1. **On-the Page Optimization:** This is work you do on the individual pieces of content that you create, whether it's a web page for your website, an article for your blog, or a video. There are things you'll need to do on those pages to communicate effectively to the search engines.

2. **Off-the-Page Optimization:** This is what you're doing in the World Wide Web at-large to effectively communicate to the search engines the relevancy of what your website or web content is really about. This is SEO at a high level.

What is SEO 2.0?

I've talked about social media as a revolution, but SEO 2.0 is more of an evolution. It is evolving to adapt to the changing type of content that's being produced today. SEO 2.0 is leveraging social media to improve your ability to communicate to the search engines about how relevant your company is in relation to your keyword phrases. SEO 1.0 was like a whisper. Before the advent of social media, you didn't have much of an opportunity to communicate as loudly as you can today. Now, thanks to the proliferation of social media, SEO 2.0 is like using a megaphone.

What is the Purpose of SEO 2.0?

The number one goal of SEO 2.0 should be to produce high rankings in the major search engines and social search. Take a look at this graph from a study conducted by a company called Enquiro. It's an eye analysis study that shows where people are more likely to look on a search result page.

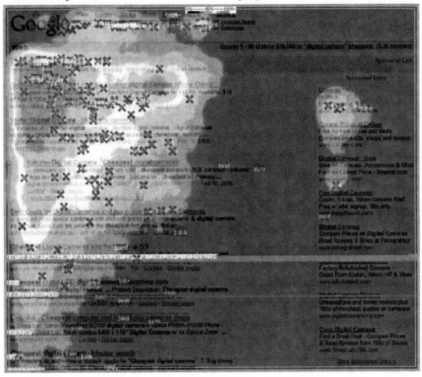

Enquiro utilized eye-tracking technology to monitor where the participants' eyes focused on Google search result pages. They discovered that people are more prone to look at the top left of a page first before shifting their focus to other areas of the page. Obviously, your goal should be to try and be in the top left position on a search results page for as many key phrases that are relevant to your content and the words your customers use when they search. If you can't be in the red spot as shown in this graph, you certainly want to be somewhere on the left side of the first page of Google.

Also notice where people look on the right side of the page. There is very little visual activity on the pay-per-click side. If you're planning to use a pay-per-click strategy, you need to be at the very top right of the page because there is very little opportunity for activity beyond that point.

The search engines have made many changes to better understand and interpret the social conversation as it influences search rankings. What I've seen over the past year is search engines like Google are beginning to play favorites with social media content. This is great news for you because you have more control over your rankings than ever before! If you produce a steady diet of social media content, such as blog articles, videos, or press releases and they're optimized for your key phrases, you're in a much better position to rank on the first page of a major search engine like Google than even your website.

However, if you want to keep your business on the first page of a major search engine like Google, you have to continue to produce social media content on a routine basis. I'll talk more about the amount of content in each of the different platform chapters. In essence, you have to produce a steady diet of content that's optimized, relevant and useful to your target audience. You'll find your company will be able to maintain a prominent position for some of your important key phrases, but it may not be the same piece of content, and that's a big difference between SEO 1.0 and SEO 2.0. In SEO 1.0, if you have a good ranking for your website for a particular key phrase with little competition from other websites, you'll stay in that position or move up or down only a few spots. With SEO 2.0 you can stay in a prominent position if you continue to publish useful, highly-optimized content.

Another purpose of SEO 2.0 is to generate traffic to your website, blog, and YouTube channel because you have those prominent positions in the search engines. What good is a top position if nobody clicks on your content? In addition, SEO 2.0 helps you build awareness so your company or brand can be exposed to people who don't know you exist. The goal is to build community with those people and get them to friend and follow you and connect with you.

The final purpose of SEO 2.0 should always be to help you grow sales through your business, either by selling a product directly or generating leads or opportunities for you through search.

Due to the technical nature of unlocking the secrets of SEO 2.0 and because I didn't want to bog you down with the details unless you wanted them, I've created a reference section entitled, SEO Tactics - The Secret Sauce at the end of this book. In that reference section, I'll walk you through, step-by-step, how to leverage SEO 2.0 for your business by integrating the following techniques:

- **How to Conduct Effective Key Phrase Research** - Developing a sound SEO 2.0 strategy for your business starts with doing key phrase research. In the SEO Tactics - Secret Sauce reference section, I'll introduce you to a five-point strategy that will provide you with 99% of what's needed in terms of building a solid SEO 2.0 key phrase analysis for your business. The other 1% will have to come from you. You'll learn how to discover the words and phrases your potential customers type into major sites like Google when they want to understand more about your industry or products/services.

- **How to Maximize On-the-Page Optimization** – You'll learn the art of on-the-page SEO and where you should drop clues within your web content to help search engines understand how to rank you for in their search results. The good news is these clues can be added on any piece of web content, regardless of whether it's a web page on your website, an article on your blog, or a video. Those clue areas will exist in the same places every time.

- **How to Successfully Use Off-the-Page Optimization** - Search engines now consider social media content important and highly relevant. For instance, if you get a link from someone else's blog to your blog, or from a highly regarded social media network like Twitter or Facebook, this will help all of your content rank better. We'll look at strategies to maximize the relevance of your content within various social networks.

- **How to Integrate Link Building Basics** - There are lots of ways to build links to your content on your own that will help you rank better in the search engines. I'll show you how to comment effectively, use link bait, and other behind the scenes tactics that will build links to your social media content.

The good news for you, as a business owner, is that if you can learn to apply the strategies detailed in the Secret Sauce reference section, you'll be in a much better position to achieve higher rankings in the search engines.

If your company has never been able to rank well in the search engines, the things you'll learn will set you in the right direction to finally get the rankings you desire. If, on the other hand, your company has been ranking well for a long time but you notice that your rankings are starting to erode, you'll be able to apply these tips and techniques to help you resurrect your results or preserve the ones you have.

5. SOCIAL MEDIA STRATEGY

Imagine you have to drive from Dallas to St. Louis and you have never driven there before and you couldn't use a map or look at any highway signs. You'd probably have a good idea where St. Louis is relative to Dallas and you'd start heading north. Eventually you would have to answer some pretty important questions such as, *When should I turn toward the East? Will this road go far enough? Am I even heading in the right direction?* That's what strategic planning is designed to eliminate. Through proper strategic planning, you will identify a purpose and destination, create a map, and determine a route and how you'll get there. Strategic planning will also help you consider who you'll take along the way.

Even that day on the Sabine River, my brother-in-law Steve had a strategic plan, albeit just a loose one, in his head. He knew what his desired outcome was, exactly where he was going on the river, what tools and resources he needed, and finally, who he was bringing along with him. This knowledge gave him the ability to have a great time on the river that day. You know what they say, "even a bad plan is better than no plan at all."

Over the past decade, I have created a process to help walk companies through strategic planning that sets them up for success in the online world. This chapter is based on that process and to begin you'll need to understand where social media fits in the world of Internet marketing.

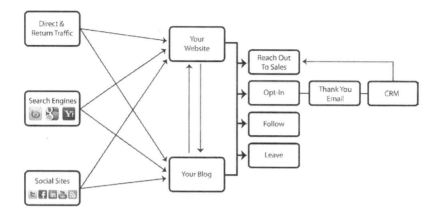

In my opinion, almost all strategic planning points toward finding and acquiring new customers. When you take a hard look at your corporate objectives, don't they always boil down to getting more people to say "yes" and buying products and services from you so your business will grow? Internet marketing serves the same purpose. The image above is a map of how customer engagements happen online. It is important to understand this map because you will use it to determine your route, help analyze where you are, and hone in on where you should focus your attention when things get off track. When it comes to Internet marketing, there are three channels or lanes people will use to engage with your business.

1. **Direct or Return Traffic.** This is when an individual has bookmarked your website or has received marketing collateral (business card from a salesperson, brochure, newspaper ad, etc.), or heard about your business in some way and they visit your website. Direct or return traffic to your site should increase over time. People may become aware of your business through the other channels (i.e.: social

sites or search) but when they return, they will most likely just type your website or blog address into their browser.

2. **Search Engines.** One of the most important channels to leverage for growing sales is search. In North America alone there are over 25 billon searches conducted within search engines every single month. This offers huge potential for companies who know how to become visible in this channel. That's why I dedicated a whole chapter on how to make your content as search engine friendly as possible. The visitors you receive from search should also grow over time. You'll also want the phrases that are being used to find your business align with the targeted key phrases you've used when optimizing your web content.

3. **Social Media Sites.** Social media sites such as Twitter, Facebook, LinkedIn, and YouTube also help customers find you and drive traffic to your business website. You'll develop strategies to grow followers and entice them to visit you. This traffic should also grow over time.

When your potential customers land on your website or your blog, four things could happen.

1. **Leave instantly.** Visitors can land on your blog or website, gather the information they need and exit, or they could decide that you're not relevant to what they were hoping to find and quickly leave. Think of your site as a leaky bucket. Part of developing a solid Internet marketing strategy will be to identify and monitor where the holes are within your site and plug them up with better content and calls-to-action. Website abandonment is when visitors land somewhere within your environment and hit the back button before

clicking to a deeper page. This is also known as bounce rate. You'll want your bounce rate decrease over time.

2. **Decide to follow you.** Regardless of how and where someone finds you it's important to make it easy for them to follow you. Make sure you have links to Twitter, Facebook, LinkedIn, YouTube and RSS feeds easily accessible on all of your Internet platforms.

3. **Opt-in.** A visitor can decide to request additional information from you by filling out a form, registering for an event, or downloading value-based content. A well-optimized environment should expect 2%-10% of visitors to opt-in. There are two types of potential buyers who will connect with you this way, which I discuss later in the book. For now it's important to understand that once someone has opted-in, you'll need to nurture them over time with useful information and multiple touches to turn these potential buyers into customers.

4. **Reach out to Sales.** Some visitors will decide to pick up the phone and reach out to your sales department, ask a question or make a purchase. Make it easy for them by putting your phone number in a highly visible place on every page of your site, blog, and social media platform. This will prevent them from having to dig for the information and cause you to potentially lose sales. This is another area where you should see an increase over time. Many Splash Media clients use call-tracking software so they can monitor the number of calls they receive from their website and via social media. Over time these calls should not only increase, but the quality of leads produced should improve as you continue to tweak and hone your messaging.

When developing a social media business plan it's important to be mindful of this process and all the different ways to target and engage your audience. The best way to do this is to identify, define and document what winning looks like for your business. I recommend you download the free Strategic Internet Questionnaire available at SplashMedia.com/Resources. This is a clear and concise resource guide that walks you through critical questions you need to be asking yourself in order to determine what winning looks like for your business.

Your Three-Legged Stool for Success

Any great strategy starts with laying a solid foundation and your social media marketing plan is no different. Just like with SEO 2.0, there is a three-legged stool and each leg is a critical component to developing a successful strategy for your business. These three legs include **defining** your goals and objectives, **measuring** your performance against those goals and objectives, and then **refining** those goals. Let's look at each of these in detail. Just like any three-legged stool, these three elements work together to achieve a common purpose. Remove one of these legs and the whole strategy can fall apart. You can't refine your strategy without measuring and you can't measure without defining what to measure.

First Leg: Define

The first step in developing a successful social media marketing strategy for your business is to identify, define, and document your goals and objectives. Over the next few pages, I outline a process and point you to resources that will help you think through this critical step in strategic planning.

Begin by considering your corporate objectives. This is one of the first questions we ask in the questionnaire resource mentioned earlier in this chapter. Social Media must tie into these objectives to lay a proper foundation for success. Corporate objectives represent the highest priority for your company during the next 12 months.

Business owners often struggle with differentiating a corporate objective from a marketing objective. Recently, I was in Washington. D.C. training a group of business owners and I asked everyone to share with the group their corporate objectives. One participant said, "To make my phone ring." When I asked her why she wanted her phone to ring, she said, "Because when my phone rings I make more sales." Then I asked her why she wanted to make more sales and her answer was to make more money. I followed up with one last question, "Why do you want to increase revenue?" Her response was perfect, "Because businesses must grow or get smaller and I want my business to grow." I said, "Perfect! You now have your corporate objective, to grow your business! All we need to do now is figure out by how much you want to grow your business." Her answer was to grow her business by 50%. I then explained to the class that this owner had just worked out a lot of her objectives:

- Grow revenue by 50%. This is a corporate objective
- Increase sales by receiving more calls from prospective customers. This is a marketing objective.

When you can answer the question *"why?"* to an objective, then you really have a lower-level objective or tactic. It turns out that "making my phone ring" was really a marketing objective, not a corporate objective. Once you can't answer *why* anymore, you are more than likely at your corporate objective. Push yourself to ask *why* until you can't anymore and this will lead to your true corporate objectives. After you've done this, we can move on to connecting these objectives to social media.

Creating Your Purpose Statement for Social Media

A key step in this first leg of the stool is to determine your purpose statement for social media. In essence, what is it you are hoping social media will do for your business? To do this effectively you'll need to connect the dots between your purpose statement for social media and your mission and value statement for your business, as well as your current overall corporate objectives. Here is a simple template to use for your social media purpose statement:

XYZ will leverage social media to [*corporate objective, or element of value statement, or mission statement*] in [*year*]. This will be accomplished by [*list high level actions-these will typically center around building community, leading with value, delivering quality content, and include your high level way to convert your audience.*]

Here is Splash Media's social media purpose statement:

Splash Media will leverage social media marketing to grow net new business by 20% [*corporate objective*] in 2011. This will be accomplished by:

- growing and nurturing our social communities
- delivering thought leadership content
- Promoting our Social Media for CEOs Boot Camps

Once you've written a purpose statement for social media in

general, I recommend you actually write a purpose statement for each of your social media channels. For instance, how will Facebook help you accomplish that purpose statement? How will LinkedIn do that? What will YouTube do to help your business? Another resource for you is a Purpose by Platform worksheet available at SplashMedia.com/Resources. This tool will help you think through how to connect these dots. It requires you to connect at least one corporate objective to a social media channel, then to consider what you will do within that channel to support your objective. Then consider what value you will deliver within the channel to your target audience and finally how you'll measure if you have succeeded. Here is an example of a purpose statement for Twitter:

> **To increase sales by:**
>
> Identifying and connecting with influencers and customers
>
> Providing useful information to nurture relationships
>
> Drawing the community to our website and blog for additional information and/or special offers
>
> **This will be measured by:**
>
> Increasing our community on Twitter
>
> The number of visitors that come from Twitter
>
> The number of Twitter visitors that respond

It will be difficult for you to succeed if you cannot connect these dots because at some point if you can't answer the question "why am I writing this blog again?" or "why am I spending time following people on Twitter?" you'll eventually give up. However, if you can focus on how these actions are helping you achieve your corporate objectives, mission, and values then you'll have the staying power needed to succeed.

Making a Comparative Analysis

As a business owner you know how much any new venture will cost you before you start to lay the foundation for a well-structured plan. The same is true for social media marketing.

How would you like to put social media marketing on a quota and *know* exactly how many new customers you will need to produce from your efforts for social media marketing to make sense? The easiest way to accomplish this is with a comparative analysis. For your convenience I have included a comparative analysis tool as part of the Strategic Internet Questionnaire in the resource section of the Splash Media website. This tool will take you through a series of questions about all the different ways you're currently spending marketing dollars and the outcomes of those marketing dollars in terms of leads or sales. It walks you through an equation to help you determine your current cost per lead or cost per acquisition. To come up with your social media quota, take your social media expenses, for example the dollars you're paying individuals within your organization or outside consultants, as well as, any advertising dollars you're planning to spend within the various social channels, and divide them by your current cost per lead or acquisition. For example, if you are planning on spending $3,000 per month on social media marketing and your current cost per lead is $100, you would divide $3,000/$100. Social media marketing will need to achieve 30 leads per month to be equivalent to what you've done in the world of traditional marketing. You wouldn't be reading this book if you didn't already know traditional advertising is eroding and therefore comparing social media marketing to your previous advertising expenditures is an early stage benchmark to get a good overall picture of your future outcomes.

Who is Your Target Market?

Another key step in the Define leg is to determine your target market. When it comes to social media, your target market has a much further reach than traditional marketing, as well as different visible players. Just like in the past, your present customers are the low-hanging fruit of your marketing efforts. In addition, people who because of what they do or their interests are also potential customers for you. What makes social media marketing unique is your target market also includes influencers. These are the people who are online talking about your industry in social media and whose followers are your current and potential customers. These influencers may be partners or vendors you are currently working with who are stakeholders in the success of your business. They could also be competitors. Yes, I just said that one of your targets in social media could be your competitors. I told you early on that social media marketing is the upside-down and inside-out world of marketing.

Each of these groups is valuable to your success and it is important that you identify them in your social media business plan, understand where and how they are using social media so you can engage with them. Where are they spending time? What sites are they visiting and commenting on? This knowledge will help you manage your time as well as the content you need to create and share. For instance, if your industry and your customers are engaging on LinkedIn more so than Facebook, you'll spend more of your time in LinkedIn.

You might consider breaking your target audience into

primary and secondary audiences. For example, customers and prospective customers might be your primary audience and influencers like partners, vendors, and competitors would be a secondary audience. Once you have broken them into groups, you should consider what your desired actions would be, by target audience. Actions by audience could be things like:

- Following you
- Visiting your website or blog
- Liking or sharing your content
- Opting-in for an event or for premium content.
- Requesting a quote or ordering a product

Identifying Social Media Profiles

There are different types of users within social media. Your target audience, regardless of whether they are customers, potential customers or influencers will utilize social media differently. Let me define the different ways people engage social media to help you understand the varying behaviors. This will help you determine desired actions by audience. Forrester Research has defined the different profiles as Creator, Critic, Joiner, Spectator, and Inactive. Let's take a look at each.

Creator: At the top of the social media food chain is the creator, which is someone who creates social media content. Creators write blogs that typically exist inside of an environment they own or control. They can also create videos or video blogs (vlogs) they share within their blog site, on YouTube, and as podcasts through iTunes, etc. By following the approach outlined in this book, becoming a creator is in your future.

Critic: The critic is someone who creates social media content but they publish it in someone else's environment, typically as comments to blogs or other social media content. This is a person who may not have a blog themselves but is active in others' blogs or they are commenting on forums or even going to sites such as Trip Advisor and talking about vacation destinations, accommodations, and restaurants they enjoyed or didn't like. Critics don't just write bad things; they are primarily expressing their opinion. Think of it like a movie critic. You will also need to become a critic. This will be critical to your success!

Joiner: The joiner is a person who has a social media profile, like a Facebook profile or a LinkedIn profile, and they update their profile periodically. These are individuals who will follow you and read your social media content. You will also be able to gain a lot of insight about what people are interested in by watching what they post.

Spectator: Spectators are people who are absolutely involved in social media today but they don't yet have a profile and they may never have one. They're watching YouTube videos or they're reading blogs. They may never create social media content as a creator or a critic, but they're absolutely part of your target audience. I encourage you to not forget about spectators. Just because they don't have profiles doesn't mean you won't be able to reach them through social media.

Inactive person: This is a person who you won't be able to reach through social media because they're not involved online. A very small percentage of your target audience would hit this category so you'll have to reach them some other way.

Conducting Competitive Analysis

Another thing you need to do in defining your goals and objectives is a competitive analysis. You need to understand what your competitors are doing. Are they on Twitter, Facebook, LinkedIn, etc.? What are they saying to their target audience? What type of content are they creating? How many fans and followers, etc. do they have? A terrific benefit of social media is that it is truly open. You can easily learn from your competitors by watching and measuring them. You can find your target audience by looking at their followers. At this stage of the process, check out your active competitors and note the following:

- What social media platforms are they utilizing?
- How many fans/followers do they have?
- How much content are they producing (i.e.: number of blogs per month and/or videos per month)?

Who Are Your Contributors?

Contributors are the subject matter experts within your organization who help you create social media content. It may be you, but I hope it's not *just* you. I hope you have product managers, technicians, customer service people and other key contributors who can help engage in the conversation and create social media content for your company.

Second Leg: Measure

Within your social media business plan you also want to determine how and what to measure. The easiest and most obvious would be to determine and measure activity. How many blogs per month do you want to publish? How many Facebook status updates? How many Twitter posts are you going to do on a monthly basis? When we look at each of the major social media platforms, I'll give you suggestions on the appropriate amount of activity to consider. Document these in advance so you can see if you are getting off track once you begin the process.

You'll also want to measure results. Here are a few general social media metrics that you might consider measuring against.

1. The growth in unique visitors to website and blog.
2. How many contest sweepstake entries you have.
3. The number of people who download or redeem coupons.
4. The number of views of your YouTube video and total views within your YouTube channel.
5. How many times your company or products are being mentioned through social media.
6. The number of comments posted, either in your social media channels or on your blog.
7. How many friends, fans, and followers you have.
8. How many times is your content reposted, Liked or Re-tweeted.
9. The number of inbound links your website or social media environment is generating.
10. The amount of inbound traffic you're receiving from social media.

All of these items can be easily measured and documented. Set goals for where you expect to be each month and compare your results with those goals. Also take a baseline of the things you can find out about your competitors. This will help you continue down the path of doing social media marketing. You'll be able to measure against where you started, where your competitors started, and how you're stacking up against their growth. We will be going into much more detail regarding what and how to measure results in Chapter 17.

Third Leg: Refine

The refinement leg is a critical element of your strategy that will propel your social media campaign in the intended direction. By following the steps outlined in this chapter, you will develop a sound social media business plan that will serve as a road map you can measure against. This leg of the process will need to be reviewed monthly. First, you'll want to set new goals in the areas where you are exceeding initial expectations. It's important to raise the bar and push yourself further when you are achieving certain measurable targets such as cost per lead, cost per acquisition, and number of fans/followers per month, etc.

Next, take a look at those areas where you're not achieving set goals and where you're missing the mark because that will enable you to manage by exception and really hone in on certain areas of your marketing efforts. This process will force you to ask the difficult questions of why it is not working the way you had hoped, and how do I fix this. By asking yourself these questions, you'll come up with solutions and changes you can implement that will likely improve your situation.

To help you continue to refine you social media business plan, consider what I call the hierarchy of needs below:

Company's Needs Hierarchy

How will your social media strategy meet these needs?

Social Media can impact each of these company needs. The easiest ones to influence are toward the bottom, with the more challenging—and valuable—needs toward the top. Continually challenge your team to move up this hierarchy. Identifying your target audience like prospects and influencers is important, but that's kindergarten. Generating leads for your business through social media is like playing on the varsity team in high school. Growing your bottom line by producing more profit for your business, now that's the major leagues! You can get there, I promise. It requires following the steps outlined in this chapter and continually refining your strategy.

If you have other individuals performing the work for you within your organization, this refinement leg will be your primary management tool. It will enable you to easily monitor your progress and hold your team accountable.

Failing to plan is planning to fail. You now have the information needed to complete a best-in-class social media business plan for your company. I encourage you to invest the time now to start building your strategy and laying the foundation for success. If you jump into social media marketing without a plan, you might luck into some short-term success, but you will never fully reach your potential. I'm not saying it's easy, but it is definitely necessary. If you follow these steps you will greatly improve your chances and reduce the amount of energy and effort

Social Rules - Social Media Strategy:

Rule #1: You must connect social media objectives with company objectives or your strategy will fail.

Rule #2: Create a social media marketing purpose statement and statements for each of your social media platforms.

Rule #3: Determine who will be your target market and spend most of your time in the platforms where they spend time.

Rule #4: Develop an action plan that identifies how many broadcasts, blog articles, and videos you plan to publish each month.

Rule #5: Create measurable goals for your social media marketing efforts to gauge progress (how many friends and followers, number of inbound links and blog mentions, social media traffic and leads, etc.).

Rule #6: Evaluate your progress and make adjustments based on success or areas of improvement.

6. RULES OF ENGAGEMENT

This is an important chapter because up until this point I've talked a lot about tactics and strategy and how you can extend your marketing message and the culture of your company into the social media landscape. However, it is also critical when you do go out into the social networking world, that you engage with people in the most effective and respectful way possible.

What are those unspoken truths about the correct way to conduct yourself or represent your company through social media? I want to give you some pointers that really dive into the proper behaviors. It all ties back to two things: people do business with people, and people love to buy, but hate to be sold. These fundamental truths don't change just because you're online. If you keep these truths in mind, following these rules of engagement will become clear.

1. Avoid Narcissism

Have you ever met or worked with people who are so self-absorbed and shallow that you don't want to be around them? All of us probably have a slight habit of being more concerned about our needs and wants than those of the people around us. When it comes to marketing your brand through social media, serving your own interests first will ultimately not serve you at all. However, helping customers achieve what they need and want will also help you succeed through social media.

When I was in sales, one truth I learned very early on was that if I was going to have a successful career, my number one goal needed to be helping as many of my customers solve their problems as I could and the rest of it would take care of itself. It turned out to be 100% true. I never once had to worry about making my quota if I focused first and foremost on helping customers. Sometimes solving their problems meant not selling them a product or service at all; it meant connecting them with a company that could better meet their particular need. My genuine concern for their success was not always tied directly to making money, but rather it was about building a long-term relationship. Honesty, humility and helping others are still the best approach.

Here are some simple ways to put others first:

- **Extend a simple "thank you."** When people decide to connect with you on Twitter, Facebook or other social media platform, take the time to thank them for following you. You'll make a great first impression if your message to them includes their first name and not just their social media account name.

- **Learn who they are.** Take the time to learn about your followers because they're more than a number. It's not about building 10,000 followers on Twitter or Facebook; it's about engaging with human beings and using social media as the medium for that engagement.

- **Remember that it's their movie, not yours.** They are the star of the movie and you are playing a supporting role. Market by anticipating their needs, and then reach out and meet their needs before they even realize they have them.

- **Be open with your knowledge and expertise.** Always lead with value without expecting reciprocity.

- **Don't manipulate or exaggerate.** Used car salesmen have a bad reputation because many have used deceptive business practices to make a quick sale. They are not worried about selling to the same customer again. However, your reputation online is written in ink. Sites like RipOffReport.com exist to give consumers a chance to fight back at companies who don't deliver or make exaggerated claims. Your motives should be about engaging in honest business practices and making not just one sale through manipulation or exaggeration, but many sales to happy, loyal customers

2. Stay Focused

There is infinitely more opportunity to get involved in conversations in various social media platforms than any one business should try to tackle out of the gate. Start with the sites discussed in this book and remember, just because you can do something doesn't mean you should. You really need to be thoughtful about your strategy and the tactics you've deployed, and avoid Social Media Attention Deficit Disorder. There's plenty of opportunity for you to fall into that trap and have your hands in so many baskets you don't accomplish anything. You want to focus on a handful of platforms or tactics that really hone your skills before you try something new. Think of it as your social media evolution. You should get really good at crawling before you walk and great at walking before you run. If you try to run first, you will stumble and fall many times without making any progress.

3. Discover Your Niche

It's really important for you to understand the concept of "me too" is never a good marketing strategy, and it really doesn't work in the world of social media. Spend time understanding what your niche is and what makes your company a monopoly. Determine what it is that your company offers customers that they cannot get from any other business. Hone your message so you can develop and clearly communicate what your unique selling proposition really is, then eloquently weave this message into social media conversations.

During initial meetings with new clients, I've asked them what makes their company unique or what's their unique selling proposition, and they tell me it is great customer service. That's not a unique selling proposition. Great customer service is a prerequisite in social media if you're going to succeed. What makes you different from your competition? What sub-segment of your industry or target market can you serve better than any other company? These questions will challenge you to dig a little deeper and identify your niche and communicate it through social media. Be prepared to prove it by living it. Your niche is not something you make up and aspire to become. It's truly part of the makeup and fabric of your company. A niche can be a segment of the marketplace or a technological advantage you have. For example, at Splash Media, some of the things that make us unique are:

- $5.5 Million Studio. We leverage this advantage by producing a weekly video blog. We also use the studio to produce monthly corporate videos for our clients as part of our social media outsourcing service—at no additional charge.

- Social Media Experience. To date, there is no other company we can find that has clocked as many man-hours actually practicing social media. We are well into the tens of thousands of hours delivering hands-on social media services at this point and growing by more than 5000 hours per month. That experience means our clients are able to tap into knowledge that would take years to replicate on their own.

- **Free Educational Seminars.** Most every week a team from Splash Media is in a major city across the country, delivering a 90-minute educational seminar. We spend well over $2 million per year putting on these events, but we know part of our role in this new media is to evangelize the importance and significance that social media will have on companies and our society.

Once you make a claim, you better be prepared to back it up with customer testimonials or success stories that validate you are the best in the business at that particular item.

4. Participate in the Conversation Outside of Your Environment

Social media isn't communication in a silo. This means going out and commenting on the blogs of your customers and potential customers as well as blogs of stakeholders, partners, vendors, and thought leaders in your space. Also participate in conversations going on within their Facebook pages, Twitter pages, and LinkedIn groups. Remember what I mentioned earlier about taking the advice of Dale Carnegie by first participating in these conversations to add value and show you are genuinely interested in the discussion. It's when you are interested in them that they become interested in you.

I recommend you participate in the conversations happening in other people's environments at least three to four times per month. This could mean responding to comments within an industry blog article or forum, posting a link to a great resource you found on the web that adds value to the conversation, or coming to the rescue and defending the argument of the author if someone tries to make him look bad.

5. Activate Customers and Employees

Get your customers on board with your social media activities by giving them a reason to participate. Communicate the value and how you'll improve their circumstance or knowledge by having them connect and engage with you and participate in the conversation. Also get your employees active in the social media environments because in many ways they are subject matter experts within their domain of responsibility inside your company. The average person on Facebook has 130 fans; therefore, every one of your customers and employees who connect with you exposes you to 130 people who may not otherwise know about you. **Give Random Acts of Kindness**

Beyond leading with value, look for opportunities to share and be kind to people you're engaging with in the world of social media. Think in terms of rewarding people who help you. A simple thank you goes a long way in the world of social media and it doesn't cost you anything. For instance, if somebody connects with you on Twitter, you can mention them in a tweet, you can go and like them on Facebook, and you can connect with them on LinkedIn. Helping your followers build their community and letting them know you care is a good way to deliver kindness.

Reward people with a little company-branded swag (baseball cap, travel mug, etc.) if they tell others in their social media network about the positive experiences they have had with your organization. Also, randomly give away cool and fun rewards to your community for just participating. Free tickets to a ballgame or a big concert coming to town go a long way toward building an active, vibrant community.

6. Educate, Educate, Educate

Customers hate to be sold, but they love to buy. You can train your customer to buy from you by giving them the information they need to formulate their buying criteria and make an informed buying decision. "Buy now!" "Buy from me!" and other forms of marketing speak don't work in the world of social media. In fact, Opinion Research Corporation conducted a recent survey and they discovered 63% of those surveyed consulted online news or blogs or consumer feedback before making a purchase. Giving information to potential customers that will help them make an informed decision is far more important than talking about you and what makes your company great. Be seen as a resource to educate customers, not sell to them.

Think about the last time you purchased a product and you used the Internet to help you make your decision. My guess is you went to the web at the beginning of the buying process to research and learn about all the features that were available. From there you formulated your buying criteria by ranking those features from most important to least important. Once you had your "must-have" features in place, you probably used the web to find the best deal. Your customers go through the same process, and if all you're doing is shouting "Buy from me!" you are missing out on a lot of opportunities and margin. I would rather engage with a potential customer at the beginning of the sales cycle so I can help them determine which features are most important. By educating them, I am also building trust and helping them buy (which is what they love to do) from me.

7. Ask Open-Ended Questions

One of the best ways to start a conversation in your social media environments is to ask open-ended questions. For instance, one of the techniques I've found to be very effective is when somebody follows me on Twitter I'll often start a dialogue. I'll start by checking out their profile page or even their blog to learn a little bit about them so when I @reply back a tweet thanking them for following me, I can ask them about their subject matter and expertise. I might also ask them a question about one of their recent tweets. When they do respond, their tweet back to me will be seen by thousands or hundreds of thousands of their followers, which is a great way to get new followers, organically.

I receive many followers from people who attended one of the Splash Media Social Media for CEOs Boot Camps. They often say something like "Loved your boot camp." I take that as an opportunity to start a dialogue by commenting back with an open-ended question. For example; "Glad you enjoyed the boot camp. What was your favorite part?"

Also consider ending your own blogs or other posts with an invitation to engage such as, "We'd love to know your opinion about this, what do you think?" It will be easy to get your community to share their opinions if you write about a controversial topic within your industry and ask people to share their thoughts. Even a simple Facebook status update that asks a question will spur community involvement. Once you have about 500 likes to your company page, you'll be surprised by the amount of response and engagement you'll receive by asking open-ended questions.

8. Assess the Time Needed and Then Commit

To represent your brand the right way and get solid engagement from the community you've developed, you have to invest the time and stick with it. Don't jump into it until you've thought through how you'll make it fit into your calendar. If you're a business-to-business (B2B) company, plan to be visible in social media every business day. If you're a business-to-consumer (B2C) company, you'll want to be present in your social media environments every single day of the week.

There is nothing worse than what I call a social media ghost town; that's when someone starts a blog but hasn't written a new entry in six months. Or, you go to somebody's Facebook page and they haven't responded to a comment on their wall in a month or more. That's much worse than doing nothing at all. I recommend you produce at least one blog every single week and try to post inside your various social media sites at least once a day. You also need to be prepared to respond to questions or comments in a timely manner. Response times should be within the same day of the post, at the latest. All of these activities shouldn't take more than 4-10 hours per week. If you do these things and make the time commitments, you'll be very happy with the results you generate.

9. Don't Give Up

I saved this one as the very last rule of engagement, because if you're like most companies, you'll reach a point when you just want to throw in the towel. You'll start to think social media will never get the return you hoped it would. You need to fight that desire to give up because typically what people base that on is their experience in the world of traditional marketing, which can create an immediate response. For instance, if I'm a car dealer and I run an ad in The Dallas Morning News offering a big rebate on a particular model, you can bet that weekend I'll have people walking onto my lot wanting to look at that car. That's an immediate response. Social media marketing is not like that at all; it's organic and it takes time to build.

If you're going to take this step and jump into the social media waters, just be prepared to stick with it for at least six months or more before you see real engagement and momentum. Tell yourself not to expect any serious engagement for six months, and if you continue to implement the strategies in this book, I guarantee that by the time you reach that six-month benchmark, you'll be happy with the type of engagement you're seeing in social media. You will have given birth to vibrant communities within social media, each with a life of its own. Communities like these can be worth literally millions of dollars to your business.

Also, expect it to take at least nine months or more before you generate any significant leads or sales from social media. You might get some leads and sales along the way, but if you make that the focus during the first nine months your communities will suffer and you will start sounding like a used car salesman. However, if you focus on leading with value and building communities those first nine months, you can expect social media to become an important part of your pipeline of opportunity.

One of my favorite motivational speakers is Zig Ziglar. I've seen him speak at least half a dozen times and what amazes me is this: although his presentation is almost the same every single time, he delivers it with such enthusiasm that I am always fully engaged. One of the key things he discusses is how difficult it is to build momentum with sales and business success. He uses the "prime to pump" example, and if you've ever seen him on stage you can picture him doing it. He grabs the handle of an old-fashioned well pump and he just starts pumping away, and pumping away, and pumping away. While he's doing this, he's talking about how important it is not to give up and just keep priming that pump and priming that pump. Eventually, the water starts to flow and it becomes easier to keep it flowing once the pump has been primed. The effort it took to get the water to flow is the hardest part of the process, which is also true with getting engagement and sales flowing through social media marketing. For the next six to nine months be prepared to prime the pump and don't give up, because you'll be very happy with the flow you've created.

Part 2

THE TACTICAL WHEEL

INTRODUCTION TO THE TACTICAL WHEEL

As most parents can relate, I recently played a role in teaching my oldest son how to drive. You remember how terrifying it was the first time you got behind the wheel. You felt any mistake you made would cause the whole world to collapse. If you were like me, you felt everyone was watching your every move just waiting for you to make a mistake and an improper stop at a light would make the local evening news. Think about all those things you had to remember to do. What pedal makes you go forward and which one causes you to slow down and stop? How do you signal a left or right turn? How about learning to parallel park? It was the most deadly of all elements of the dreaded driving test at the local DMV. Now think about how easy it is to drive today, and how quickly it became second nature to you. Social media marketing can seem equally daunting, but I promise you it can also become as easy as driving a car if you begin to understand the basic tactics that are required to navigate your business through the social media landscape.

The best way to get your head around social media marketing and how it's going to benefit your business is to introduce you to the Tactical Wheel. This concept integrates the tactical techniques you need to get a campaign up and running and to sustain that campaign to deliver value on an ongoing basis. The different stages of the Tactical Wheel can be implemented across all social media platforms. Just like driving a car. All cars have the same pedals and the same signals. When you learn how to drive one car, you can pretty much drive them all. My intention in developing this concept is to give you a set of universal actions you will take regardless of social media platform. First, I'll walk you through a quick, high-level overview of the Tactical Wheel and then we'll take a deep dive into each one of the pieces individually.

Entire chapters in this book are dedicated to the top five social media platforms. We will use the Tactical Wheel as a guide in each of those chapters to make it easier for you to comprehend the actions needed by each platform to move you in the desired direction.

The first component of your social media marketing campaign is to listen to the conversations taking place in social media today. What listening will do is help you identify those influencers and potential customers who are already involved in social media that you want to connect and engage with.

After you've been listening for a while you can move into *building community,* which is simply getting people to friend and follow you. Once you have spent time building community you start broadcasting. *Broadcasting* is the process of sharing and posting thoughts, opinions, and links to content within the social media communities with the purpose of communicating, helping and influencing your target audience. Broadcasting is like fishing; its primary purpose is to get people to go somewhere else, such as your website or blog. Content is the next step in the Tactical Wheel and it typically consists of content you've created for your target audience to enjoy. Your content can take the form of blog articles, YouTube videos, or discussions. It's essential that you go through the entire process of listening, building community and broadcasting to ultimately get people to land on your content. This is where you'll lead with value and train your customers to buy from you.

If you do a good job at the content stage, you'll earn the right to go to the next level with them. The litmus test for measuring whether you have added value is if readers of your content can walk away afterward and think to themselves, "That was worth three to five minutes of my day." If you feel that's how most visitors would feel, then you can move to the next step, which is to ask them to engage with you on a deeper level. Asking users to register for an event, to register and receive additional information, sign up for a program or make a purchase is what constitutes the *conversion* stage of the Tactical Wheel.

As your social media campaign grows and expands, you'll continue to follow the Tactical Wheel and spiral in a direction that will be not only useful to you, but also meaningful and beneficial to your target audience.

7. LISTENING

Did you know listening is the most effective communication skill? If you want to engage users in social media, you need to become a good listener. Listening is basically the act of identifying social media conversations around topics relevant to your business. These might be social discussions started by customers, potential customers, or even competitors. They may be industry-related conversations inside blogs and discussion groups, or posts made on Twitter, Facebook, and LinkedIn.

One of the main reasons you need to get into social media marketing now if you haven't started already is because these conversations are already happening within your industry. For many of you, there are already conversations going on in social media around the products and services that you provide, and I'll bet there are some about your very own company. These discussions are from individuals who are asking for help, giving help, sharing their opinions, offering advice, recommending companies, and ripping some apart. All you have to do to find them is to listen. Listening in to find these conversations might be simpler than you think because the world of social media is open for everyone to see.

So why is listening to these conversations so important for your business success? Here are several key reasons.

1. **To identify potential customers currently active in social media.** This includes individuals who make up your ideal prospects and who are publically talking about their

interests, needs, wants and problems they need solved. By listening to those conversations you can identify active prospects and find conversations in which you might want to contribute.

2. **To identify influencers in your industry.** They could be potential partners, competitors, or just influencers discussing your industry within social media. Find those influencers by listening so you can engage with them and offer your knowledge and expertise, as well as promote them to your communities. That's right. I just said you might be promoting competitors (and other influencers) to your own community. That probably sounds counterproductive but remember, this is the inside-out, upside-down way of marketing. This is also why you need to know your niche. Because once you do, you really won't have any true competitors and you'll be able to pull it off.

This will help you hit a major milestone in the world of social media. This milestone, or tipping point, is when other people start sharing your content or talking about your products and services in the social media platforms. One of the easiest ways to get other people to start talking about your business is to find people who are already communicating about your industry. Once you help them accomplish what they need, they'll start talking about you, too.

3. **To identify and reward happy customers.** If you haven't already, you'll soon have customers talking about positive experiences they've had with your brand online, and you'll want to reward them. It's important to let them know that, (1) you heard them and (2) you appreciate their business. A

win for your happy customers is when you acknowledge them and say thanks for the business.

4. **To identify content to curate and share with your community.** Most influencers use social media to promote their original content to their followers. If you recall, the primary role in social media is to be a creator, someone who creates social media content. Listening will enable you to find relevant content from other people that would be useful to your followers. You then will be able to act as a curator and share this content to your community.

5. **To identify and shift unhappy customers into happy customers.** You'll be able to find unhappy customers through listening to their conversations and complaints. You can then address their issues by taking the conversation offline. You can apply the process I outlined in the Reputation Management section that deals with turning negative experiences into positive ones.

Here's a story that really drives home the value of listening. One of the reasons I live in Dallas is because it's in the south and I'm not a big fan of cold weather. While Dallas typically has mild winters, I look for an opportunity to go to a warmer climate, for business or pleasure, sometime during the colder months. A couple of winters ago, right after Dallas was hit with a record snowfall, I had an opportunity to go on a business trip in the Miami area. The meeting was scheduled for a Monday morning so I decided my wife and I should make a full weekend out of the opportunity to be in a much warmer climate and escape the snow.

I didn't know where I wanted to stay but I did have two buying criteria. One was to stay on the beach; if I was going to go all the way to Florida, I wanted to make sure I was on the beach—no matter what. Number two, I wanted to pay as little as possible. Like most people in the early stages of a buying process, I decided to use Google to find hotels along the Atlantic coast near Miami. Using Google Maps, I started bouncing from one hotel listing to the other until I found a listing for the following hotel that I thought was interesting, so I checked out their website.

As you can see by the home page of their website, the hotel was on the beach, which addressed my first buying criteria. As I dug a little bit deeper into the website, I discovered that their rates were 20% less than any other site I'd looked at to that point, which satisfied my second criteria. I was just about to book a reservation with them when, at the last second, I decided to check out TripAdvisor.com to see if there was anything written about the hotel that might influence my buying decision.

On the TripAdvisor.com site I typed in the name of the hotel and, as you can see by the graphic below, the very first review says it's a great place to stay *if* you like bedbugs.

Like you, I'm not a big fan of bedbugs, so I decided not to stay at that particular hotel. That's one of the key points about listening. No longer did the fact that they were right on the beach matter. No longer did the fact that they were 20% less than any other hotel I'd looked at so far matter. One person's comment is all it took for that company to lose a sale. I have no idea who that person was; for instance, it could have been a disgruntled employee who was laid off that morning. What did matter to me was not taking my wife on a three-day weekend and risking the possibility of sharing our mini-vacation with bedbugs.

How many sales has this company lost because they are not listening to the conversation going on in social media? If they were listening, they could have responded to this reviewer and reminded him/her that bedbugs are a huge problem, and provided links to recent news stories. They could have shared the fact that bedbug infestation often starts with guests who bring them onto the property from their own homes. Then, taking responsibility for the problem, they could have explained that they spent $10,000 to fumigate the hotel and the inspectors gave then a clean report. Finally, they could have invited the reviewer back to stay for free.

This is exactly why it's important to get in the social media game. You can't just put your head in the sand and hope this stuff will go away. The act of listening will help you see when those types of comments or conversations are happening so you can deal with them and fix them.

How to Actively Listen

When it comes to actively listening in order to put your best brand forward, there are a few steps you need to take.

Key Phrase Research

The critical first step in listening is to compile key phrase research. This will help you understand which words and phrases your customers and potential customers are using to search within your industry to formulate their buying criteria. (This was covered in great detail in the SEO 2.0 chapter. Be sure to watch the video resource to help you develop a powerful key phrase analysis for your business.) With your key phrase analysis, you are now equipped to start listening to conversations.

Best Ways to Listen

There are several effective and *efficient* ways to listen for your keywords and phrases online:

Boolean Searches: You can use different Boolean searches as a reference, and an extensive list of Boolean searches is included in the Appendix of the book to help you along the way.

Google Alerts: One of the best ways to listen is to set up Google Alerts and connect the alerts to your iGoogle Reader and make the Reader your home page. This way, whenever you log into Google, you'll be able to see all the real-time conversations about particular key phrases by source. It makes it very easy to just listen and monitor the conversations.

STEP 1

STEP 2

STEP 3

STEP 1: Set up Google Alerts
STEP 2: Select Deliver to Feed
STEP 3: Add it to iGoogle and make iGoogle your home page.

Twitter: Another way to listen is to go to Twitter and type those key phrases right into Twitter (with quotations on either side) and see the real-time conversation going on within Twitter. You also have the option to save that search inside Twitter, so you can monitor the conversation. However, if you have a local or regional business, you'll want to go to search.twitter.com/advanced. This will enable you to hone in your search, but most importantly it will allow you to filter by geographic location. For example, if you're a pest control company that serves only the Dallas area, you really aren't interested in people complaining about ants in New York City.

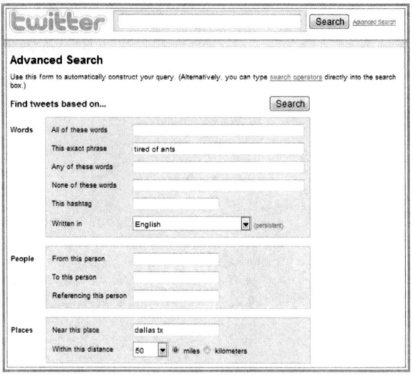

Use search.twitter.com/advanced to listen to conversations within a certain area.

SocialMention.com: SocialMention.com is a free tool that's a powerful search engine just for social media content. If you're a local or regional business, and you're only interested in conversations happening in and around the geographic community you serve, and want to see more than just tweets, Social Mention is a great way to condense your results down to the conversations that are within your geographic perimeters. You can also set up a feed for certain search results in Social Mention that you can bring into your iGoogle Reader as well and monitor it in one place.

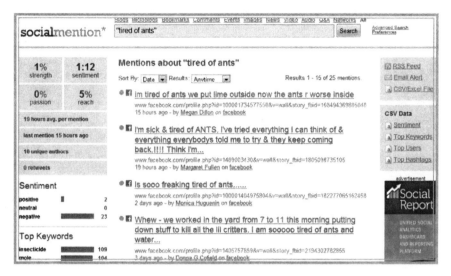

SplashCube.com: Splash Media developed a social media management tool that we use to manage our clients' social media marketing campaigns. In the fall of 2011 we made SplashCube available to the general public. One of the capabilities of SplashCube is to monitor conversations inside Twitter and Facebook from a central location. This enables you to identify key individuals by their posts and then to manage your engagement with those individuals directly from SplashCube without having to log into either Twitter or Facebook.

Industry sites and blogs: Take an inventory of all the different industry-related magazines you receive on a monthly basis and then go check out the websites of those magazines and look for articles. More important than reading every article in its entirety, you should scroll down to the bottom of the article and look at the comments. The people who make the time to comment on the article are the influencers you want to engage with, and a big part of listening is identifying influencers.

Social Rules – Listening:

Rule #7: Use Twitter Advanced Search, Google Alerts, Social Mention, and SplashCube to actively listen to conversations related to your industry.

Rule #8: Use key phrases to listen for and identify influencers and prospective customers.

Rule #9: Listen using industry terms to discover content to curate and share with your communities.

Rule #10: Use an RSS reader, such as Google Reader, to manage feeds and active conversations so they coalesce into one place.

8. BUILDING COMMUNITY

Building community is simply getting all of the people you have a common interest with to connect with you. "Connecting" means getting these individuals to "Like" your Facebook page, to follow you on Twitter, connect with you on LinkedIn, etc. This includes customers, prospects, influencers, partners, and employees. This is important for a few key reasons:

1. **Provides a direct way to communicate with your target audience.** It's like the old saying, "If a tree falls in the woods and nobody is there to hear it, does it really make a sound?" If you don't have solid communities within the key social media environments, then nobody will be around to listen when you have something to say. Have you noticed that at the end of many commercials these days the advertiser is pointing you to their Facebook page rather than their website? The reason for this is once you become a part of their community, they can effectively (and inexpensively) communicate with you. This extends the value of their commercial way beyond the 30-second spot.

2. **Helps you gain exposure to their connections.** As soon as you begin to post and communicate with those people your brand and message will be visible to everyone they are connected to as well.

3. Allows large communities to influence purchase decisions. When potential customers are making decisions about what brand to purchase or company to use, they can check out your social media environments. If you are a B2B

company and have a vibrant community on LinkedIn or a B2C company with thousands of followers on Facebook, this will influence their purchase decision.

4. Gives your customers a platform to praise and curse you. Both are good. Obviously, you want to consolidate all the good things your evangelists want to share about you and have a vibrant community that amplifies their impact. However, even negative comments in a vibrant community are good. When a negative comment is posted, often your evangelists will rise to the occasion and defend you right there in front of everyone in the social media world. When you step in to resolve an issue using the steps outlined in the Reputation Management section of this book, you are showing the world you care and are interested in making things right.

Ways to Build Community

There are a variety of ways to build community within your social media channels to connect with your target audience and get them to friend or follow you.

Send out an eBlast: One way would be to send out an eBlast to all of your customers, prospects, and partners, notifying them that you have set up social environments to better serve and communicate with them. The message needs to focus on how you plan to utilize these environments to provide enhanced customer service. Earlier in the book we discussed writing purpose statements for each social media environment. As part of that exercise, you needed to determine what value you will deliver within that platform to your target audience. You can use that value statement inside the eBlast to communicate your plans to help them via each platform.

If you send out the eBlast with the intention of making it a customer service aid, you'll build community very quickly using the email database you've been collecting over time. I also encourage you to repeat this effort every month or two by sending out another email blast to only the new addresses you've since added to your database, as well as to anyone who did not connect from the previous attempt.

Get employees involved: Because the average person on Facebook has 130 friends, every one of your employees who has a Facebook account has about 130 people that may not know very much about what products or services your company provides. Getting your employees to follow your different social media environments is a great way to (1) help your employees feel connected to the organization, which will help your retention numbers and (2) create an opportunity for you to become exposed to their followers or friends, which will help you build community with those individuals.

Add Follow Us buttons: You should also put the "follow us" icons on every page of your website, above the fold, so no one has to scroll down to find them. This is becoming a common practice because companies want to make it very easy for their visitors to use a simple click to get connected and engaged within social media. You should also add follow us information on all of the marketing and advertising methods you're using, such as direct mail, billboards, radio, print and even business cards.

For printed materials, it's important you don't just include a follow us icon; also include the actual address for your social media environment. For instance, I have seen "Follow us on Facebook" included in a newspaper advertisement but the address of the Facebook page is not listed. This puts too much burden on the reader because now they have search for you. It's better to say "Follow us on Facebook – Facebook.com/yourcompanyname." The key point to remember with social media marketing is you have to make it extremely easy for people to find you and follow you.

Here is the six-step activation process Splash Media uses to activate our clients' customers, prospects, employees, and stakeholders.

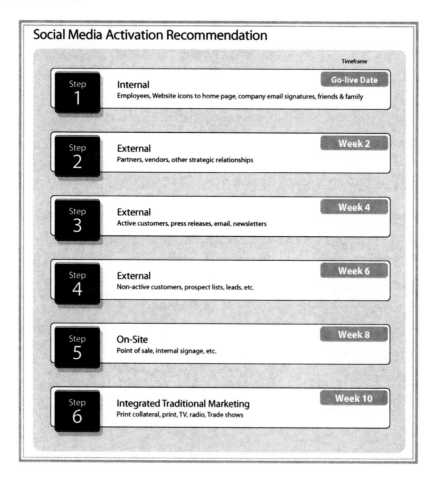

Incentivize your community through social media-only promotions and events: By offering exclusive special events or discounts that users can learn about only from social media will encourage your followers to spread the word to their friends. For example, if you own a restaurant you can create a special coupon for free drinks, or even offer a certain percentage off the bill, but the coupon is only available to people who like your Facebook page. If you make the offer available to the people who already like your page, they'll be able to get access to it and they'll tell their average of 130 friends, which will help you build community. If you are a B2B company, another example would be to host a "social media only" after-party at a trade show. To gain entrance into the after-party, guests have to bring or show on their phone a ticket that could only be accessed via social media. You could post the ticket inside your LinkedIn group, on your Facebook page, or by sending it automatically to users who follow you on Twitter.

Special note: it is important that you follow all promotional and contest guidelines of the individual social media platforms or your page may be shut down. All Facebook conditions can be accessed by clicking on the Terms link at the bottom of your Facebook page. For promotional guidelines go to: https://www.facebook.com/promotions_guidelines.php

Leverage search engine optimization (SEO): This is the number one way to build community through social media. There are infinitely more people out there who don't know you than those who do know you. Tapping into the billions of searches conducted in sites like Google each month will enable you to build community with individuals who don't know your company even exists. However, these individuals are highly qualified because they are searching for information about the products and services your company provides. This is why I devoted an entire chapter to Search Engine Optimization 2.0.

Let me explain this further by first going back to the key phrase spreadsheet list you made for creating content for social media. These keywords will be used in your blogs, YouTube videos, press releases, headline tweets and Facebook posts. These key phrases are the way your customers find you when they are trying to make informed buying decisions, formulate their buying criteria, or look for the best deal on product X. They'll use the same words you are optimizing when they search Google, Bing or Yahoo!. If you remember back in Chapter 4 I talked about the study conducted by Enquiro to monitor where people's eyes focused when viewing websites. The majority of the eyes looked at the left side of the first page of Google. Therefore, if you want to build community through search engine optimization it's paramount that your social media content shows up on the first page of a search.

The good news is Google is continually modifying the way they rank websites. Lately Google has been trying to keep up with sites like Twitter and Facebook. By their nature Twitter and Facebook offer users content in real time because the content is supplied by their users. Google, however, uses software to "crawl" the web and find relevant content, which takes more time.

A perfect example of content delivered in real time is when the announcement was made about Osama bin Laden's death. I remember sitting in bed that Sunday evening and right before the news came on television, there was an announcement that President Obama was about to address the nation at any moment but they didn't say why. I guessed it had to be pretty important, considering it was late on a Sunday night. I waited patiently during the news program, but after the anchor said for what felt like the tenth time "Stay tuned because right after this break, the President will be addressing the nation," I decided to go to Twitter and conduct a search for Obama and quickly discovered bin Laden had been killed. Think about that for a minute. I was able to learn about an important event via social media before my local news or even the President of the United States could tell me. Now that's what I call real-time information!

As a result of this type of access, it appears Google is now playing favorites with social media content. What all of this means is, if you create a blog, YouTube video or a social media post, and follow the steps outlined in Chapter 4, you have a much better shot at having that content hit the first page of Google than you would with your website. That's the good news. However, remember that social media content doesn't typically maintain a top listing for a long period of time. Google wants fresh, relevant content, so you might get a nice listing for a while but then you'll see that listing start to fall down the search results page slowly over time. It may take a week or a month, depending on how much competition exists in your industry. The key here is to produce a steady diet of relevant social media content that is highly optimized for the search engines.

Here's a quick case study about the impact of social media can have on a business and their search engine ranking. Splash Media has a client in Dallas, ElectricMan, Inc., and one of their unique selling propositions is their services are available 24 hours a day. As mentioned in the strategy chapter, understanding your niche and unique selling proposition is important in social media and obviously we wanted to promote this selling point because it would set our client apart from their competition. We created content around that concept, optimized it by using key phrases in the right places and we were fortunate enough to earn them a very high ranking on the first page of Google for the key phrase of "24-hour electrician Dallas." If you take a close look at the following screenshot you'll see the top results were not their website listing, but instead two articles from their blog.

The story doesn't end there. A week before hosting the Super Bowl in 2011, Dallas was hit with one of the worst ice storms in recent memory. We had two inches of ice and then six inches of snow on top of the ice. Because of the large number of visitors expected to arrive in Dallas for the Super Bowl, the Red Cross brought in additional blood supply, which is something they do in any city hosting the Super Bowl. In the middle of the night the Dallas Red Cross lost power during the ice storm. I am not exactly sure what the status was on their generators, but for some reason they were completely out of power and in jeopardy of losing their blood supply.

When they went to Google to search for an electrician who could solve their crisis after hours, they typed in "24-hour electrician Dallas" into the search box. They found our client, ElectricMan on the first page and gave them a call. They went out in the middle of the night, during the ice storm, fixed their problem, and saved the blood supply. As a result of their efforts, ElectricMan was featured in a Twitter post by the Red Cross in Dallas that read, "Our hero Electric Man. When power failed at 1:30 a.m. Red Cross Dallas' storage was at risk, who did they call, the Electric Man to the rescue."

From that one service call ElectricMan has experienced a significant rise in business. This was a direct result of generating social media content with targeted key phrases to leverage search engine optimization. As you can see in this next chart for ElectricMan, within the first 90 days of engaging in social media they saw a nearly 100% increase in overall search engine traffic.

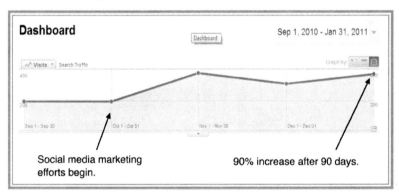

Even if your business is already ranking well in the search engines, you need to get involved in social media marketing because it will help you maintain and sustain your search engine rankings. Social media marketing is definitely one of those activities that if you follow the processes laid out in the rest of this book it will give you the opportunity to rank very well on a major site like Google. In fact, early in 2011 Larry Paige, the CEO of Google, said they were absolutely paying attention to the social media signals, and that these signals are influencing search results but that they have only touched 1% of their capability. Having a social media component to your marketing strategy will definitely help your company maintain and generate search result rankings, which is the number one way to build community through social media.

Social Rules - Building Community:

Rule #11: Make sure all of your content is search engine optimized. This is the number one way to build community with prospects that don't know you exist.

Rule #12: Use the 6-step activation process to quickly build community with customers, partners, vendors, and prospects.

Rule #13: Add Follow Us buttons to your website and marketing collateral.

Rule #14: Actively reach out to influencers and encourage them to connect with you.

Rule #15: Conduct social media-only promotions and events.

9. BROADCASTING

I recently watched a documentary about Mark Twain's history as a public speaker. His story-telling talent and humor made him a very popular attraction when he rolled into town. On one occasion, as the curtain raised and he walked out on stage, he just stared at the audience and didn't say a word. The audience looked at him and he stared right back at them. After a few minutes of extremely awkward silence, a single chuckle could be heard from the crowd and from there the audience busted out with roaring laughter. What made that work for Twain was the fact that silence between humans is uncomfortable and awkward. The social media environments you participate in are your stage and while awkward silence worked in Twain's case, it won't work for you inside these platforms. You need to get out there and communicate.

Broadcasting is simply communicating with your audience by posting information through social media. This is a big part of your contribution to the conversation. So far I've talked about how listening will help you find influencers and customers through social media. Then I explained how to build community and connect with those people. Now, broadcasting is your big opportunity to get into the conversations; to actually deliver value and communicate things that would be relevant and important to the people who are following you.

EXAMPLES OF BROADCASTING
- Facebook status update
- Twitter posts (tweets)
- LinkedIn status updates for your personal profile
- LinkedIn group discussions
- YouTube comment to a video
- Answers to questions through LinkedIn Answers or Yahoo Answers
- Commenting on other people's blogs

Purposes of Broadcasting

There are five primary reasons to engage in broadcasting within your social media environments.

1. **Drive people to your content in an environment you control.** You want to be a part of the conversation, but you need to be intentional about it because you want the people you're engaging with in social media to actually click through and end up in an environment you control, such as your website, blog or YouTube channel. I don't mean every time you post something, but understand that an overarching goal of broadcasting is to draw individuals from your social community into your other environments. As mentioned earlier, broadcasting is like fishing. You are putting information out there hoping to get these individuals to go somewhere else. Sometimes you are chumming the waters with good quality content and sometimes you throw a hook in the water with links back to you.

2. Curate useful information that will keep your followers up to date regarding your industry. You don't always have to be the author of the content, but instead you can act as the curator. You are searching out valuable and relevant information and filtering it to your followers. This strategy will serve you well as your followers are expecting you to be their adviser in your industry. Find good content by listening with key phrases and then post links within your community to the content you find helpful. If you locate an article that will garner a lot of interest, write a summary of the article in your blog with a link to the article and then post the link to your blog in your environments. This way you are drawing your community to you rather than sending them somewhere else.

3. Become exposed to followers of other industry leaders. When you comment on a non-competitive influencer's blog and you're part of their conversation, you're exposing yourself to their followers and hopefully providing value so their followers eventually become your followers.

4. Better way to communicate than email - . I believe communicating through social media directly with our fans and followers will ultimately replace email marketing. If you are anything like me you delete most of the email marketing mail that crowds your inbox without even opening them. This gives the sender very little visibility to you and zero visibility to your friends and followers.

5. However, when I log into sites like Facebook and LinkedIn I tend to open up messages and read status updates of brands and companies because their messages are on my News Feed, plus I have agreed to follow that group or

become a fan of that brand. I am a warm target audience for them and the engagement level will always be much higher than a solicitation email would receive. We already know that statistically, in terms of return on investment, that email marketing is becoming more and more difficult to create great value, whereas it is much easier to leverage connections through social media.

Best Ways to Broadcast

There are a couple of different elements to discuss here. One is what I call **scheduled broadcasts**, which are predetermined days of the week and month in which you already know you'll be promoting a particular topic, concept or call to action. It's easy to plan ahead and keep track of these broadcasts by using a content or editorial calendar and you can download the one Splash Media uses from the resource section of our website. One type of scheduled broadcast should be about promoting content such as a blog or video. For instance, you should plan to publish a blog or upload a video on a particular day and then promote it on your different social media platforms to drive traffic to the content.

Another type of scheduled broadcast would be related to upcoming events, such as an educational or promotional event, a tradeshow, a workshop or a webinar. These are all events that you should be broadcasting about, and it's easy to schedule them on your content calendar to make sure you are creating visibility and buzz around them through social media.

Seasonal posts are also easy to make into scheduled broadcasts. Practically every month of the year has different seasonal-related events, such as Mother's Day, Father's Day, holidays, and various big sporting events for which you can plan broadcasts around. To make it easy for you to plan ahead, we've added a list of possible holidays and big events that occur every month in the Appendix section of the book.

Opportunistic broadcasts are the type of broadcasts you post when an opportunity arises to either curate information, act as a social media concierge, or sell your product or service. To capitalize with opportunistic broadcast, you must be actively listening for targeted key phrases. When you're acting as a curator you're looking for articles that would be beneficial to your target audience and then reposting those within your social media environments. By listening, this is a very easy thing to do because most of the blogs and videos you'll find through searches and your iGoogle Reader will already have buttons that enable you to instantly re-publish the information through your social media channels.

Another example of an opportunistic broadcast is to share information about current events. For example, something major might happen in your industry and you want to keep your followers informed. This, in turn, helps you establish yourself as an influencer who is tuned into your industry.

Your potential customers are using social media every day. When they talk about a need or complain about an issue, this is your opportunity to either act as a concierge or jump in and try to make a sale. At Splash Media, every single week, we are helping our clients sell everything from cars, to electrical and pest control services, to reconditioned aircraft engines. If we can sell aircraft engines through social media, I am confident you'll be able to sell your products and services, too.

Therefore, **making offers** through broadcasting is another way to connect to your customers through social media. I'd like to share a quick case study with you regarding this type of broadcast. The Shops at Park Lane is a client of Splash Media and they own and manage a mixed-use high-end retail and apartment development. Indirectly, we represent all of the different stores and shops within Park Lane and we use the same process for their social media campaign as I am describing in this book.

Back in the fall of 2010 we saw this tweet from a woman who was looking for a place to eat before going to a movie at the Inwood Theater.

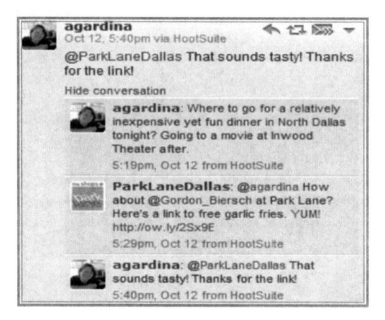

Inwood Theater happens to be a movie theater down the street from Park Lane, and because we were set up to listen for "Inwood Theater" as a key phrase in our iGoogle Reader, we were able to take quick action. As you see in the previous image, we responded to her tweet within ten minutes of its posting and we sent a reply back to her that said, "How about Gordon Biersch at Park Lane? Here's a link to free garlic fries. YUM!," and we included a shortened link to the coupon. About ten minutes later she replied back to us and said "That sounds tasty. Thanks for the link." I don't know if she was going to dinner with a girlfriend or 20 friends, but that's a classic example of an opportunistic broadcast of engaging directly with the potential customer and making an offer—an offer that was seen not only by her but also by all of her followers on Twitter.

Another great example is recently when I was sitting on an airplane and I checked in on FourSquare, which is a geo-targeted social media platform, to broadcast that I was checked into DFW Airport and looking forward to the boot camps we'd be doing up in Las Vegas. I posted that broadcast on Twitter and Facebook and two and a half hours later, when my plane landed and I turned on my phone, I already had one reply on Twitter related to my post. A VIP service was listening for the word Vegas through Twitter and sent me this reply, "Hey Paul. Hope you have a great time in Vegas. Here's my phone number. If you need a limo or anything give me a call. I'll take care of you." That VIP company was actively listening to key phrases that were related to their industry, which enabled them to engage directly with a potential customer in a matter of minutes.

Responding to conversations is another type of broadcasting that takes your engagement with potential customers to a much deeper level. Once you become active in social media and you begin to publish content and build relationships, people start communicating with you. They'll respond to content you create; they may ask your opinion about a topic or just say hello, and you need to be prepared to communicate back with them. These conversations can also be going on between other users and not necessarily directed to you, however, you can still jump into the conversation if you can add value. Don't be shy. Social media is a lot like the old party line telephones where you could hear everyone's conversation. Only in this case it's ok to jump in and share your thoughts and opinions. The low barrier to entry is one of the benefits of social media marketing.

A rule that's really important as it relates to broadcasting is what I call the 90/10 rule. Simply put, 90 % of what you broadcast should be beneficial, useful and informative to your target audience; the other 10 % of what you broadcast can be promotional. The Park Lane coupon example I mentioned earlier would only make up 10 % of their campaign. Remember: most of the broadcasts are centered on promoting content, curating content and talking about current events.

To help run your campaign in an effective and efficient way, you'll need to pick a tool to manage your broadcasts. There are three major scheduling tools out there: TweetDeck, HootSuite, and SplashCube. All three give you the opportunity to create a post and then select where you want that post to go. You could choose to broadcast a post in all of your different social media channels with one click of the button, or you could be selective and choose to have it go to just one channel or a subset of your channels. I personally use SplashCube, but have used TweetDeck in the past and have heard many good things about HootSuite. You can't go wrong with any of these.

When you're posting links to your website or to curated content use a URL shortener to help give you more space because, in most cases, you're limited to 140 characters. My recommendation is that you use Bitly.com; it's a free service where you take a long

URL, paste it into the blank space on their site and it automatically shortens the URL to typically less than ten characters. You can simply click the Copy button and then paste the shorter URL into your post. Bit.ly is a great tool because it not only shortens your URL, it also provides you with statistics about how many people have clicked on the link (called a click-through rate), where the clicks are coming from (Facebook, Twitter, etc.) and it will also show you every tweet or re-tweet using that link. This is a great way to gauge the effectiveness of your efforts and receive detailed information about who is supporting your content so that you can thank them directly.

Social Rules - Broadcasting:

Rule #16: Lead with value and become a social media concierge.

Rule #17: Remember the 90/10 rule and keep your promotional broadcasts to just 10 % of your posts.

Rule #18: Plan scheduled broadcasts around holidays, specific events, building awareness and specific promotions.

Rule #19: Be opportunistic and broadcast timely newsworthy content to curate and share with your followers.

Rule #20: Engage with in-market prospective customers in real time by responding to their requests for help.

Rule #21: Become a thought leader by answering questions.

Rule #22: Don't be shy. Jump in on conversations to start a dialogue with other social media users.

10. DEVELOPING CONTENT

In order for me to really talk about developing good, useful, beneficial social media content, I want to discuss the concept of social media currency. It's very important to understand that in the world of social media, content and engagement is about helping other people achieve their objectives and helping your potential customers make informed buying decisions. Considering your social media currency, the value you plan to use to *pay* for engagement, will help you maximize your opportunities in this media. This currency will typically exist inside the content you produce. As you think about developing social media content, you need to expand on the concept of leading with value.

How to Lead with Value

I have consulted with many businesses over the years that were terrified about putting any of their "secret sauce" or "trade secrets" on their website. They were afraid the competition would steal something valuable from them. They wanted their website to be a glorified brochure. I always told them that if they built their website as a glorified brochure, their customers and prospects would treat it the same way they do your brochure; which is to throw it in the trash. There are too many websites today that come across to the visitor as narcissistic rants about why their company is better than their competition. Here is a wake-up call. Your users don't care about you! They don't care about your company and what you sell. All they care about is themselves… Period! When they land on your website or blog they want to know very quickly how you can help them. WIIFM is king! What's-in-it-for-me, has never been more true when it comes to successful web marketing.

With the right perspective about web users, you can use WIIFM to your advantage by leveraging the narcissistic tendencies of your followers and giving them what they want and perceive as valuable. This is your social media currency. When it comes to creating valuable content for your customers, there are a few ways to do this.

Archived knowledge: This is the simplest form of social media currency if you have it, and not every business does. Archived knowledge is content that has already been created by your company. Traditionally it is just sitting on the shelf in some non-web enabled format that your potential customers would love to get their hands on when they're in the buying process or when they are trying to determine all the features available to them. Books, white papers, or case studies you have written that can be re-purposed for the web are excellent examples.

Archived knowledge could also be data that's locked up in various applications used for different purposes. For example, I recently consulted with a high-end recruiting firm that specializes in certain key hires only in Dallas. Talk about niche. They have been in business for 35 years and they place several key people in Dallas-based businesses every month. I suggested they publish a quarterly report on what the Dallas market will bear for the positions they fill by taking the aggregate information about all the placements they made in the previous quarter. With the data they currently have locked in their computers, they could easily produce a highly valuable document on compensation, benefits, etc. that would be useful not only to candidates but also employers.

Another colleague of mine owns a project management consulting practice in Dallas and he wrote a book about his field of expertise. We were having lunch one day and we were talking about this idea of social media currency. He couldn't really connect the dots until I reminded him that he wrote two books on the subject, one of which I wrote the forward. That's the type of information his potential customers would love to get their hands on when they're in the buying process. All he needed to do was take the knowledge that's locked away in that book and make it available through blog posts, downloadable chapter excerpts, etc. and his potential customers and his business would benefit from sharing his content online. Achieved knowledge could also be locked up in the heads of your subject matter experts. One of the reasons I am writing this book is to get the information in my head down on paper. Once the book is written this content can be repurposed in the form of blogs articles or videos.

Real-time knowledge: This type of knowledge is one of the most effective ways of building community and driving value through social media as it relates to content. This is where you become a thought leader in your industry and you begin to develop content and answer questions to help potential customers formulate their buying criteria. However, for this to work effectively, you need to be prepared to help everyone, even those who end up taking their business to your competition. What do I mean by this? Your intention should be to share knowledge and content in an unbiased way to help your audience make informed buying decisions in real time, while they are in market and looking for help, even if it doesn't result in a sale.

Humor: A sense of humor works well in the appropriate circumstances. You may be familiar with the Old Spice YouTube campaign. That was a very effective campaign for Old Spice, as their sales doubled. However, let me warn you, it is best to avoid building your entire social media strategy on humor with the hope of going viral because creating viral content is the most difficult form of social media currency. As I've mentioned, having content go viral is like trying to win the lottery. You just don't know if that content is going to take off the way you hope it will.

Products: You can actually use products as social media currency. Can you come up with a light version, demo version, or lost leader version of your product, and make that available through social media channels as your social media currency? Or maybe you can develop a configurator that helps your customers determine what product or solution is best for them, and then turn it into a smartphone application and make that available through social media content. For example, in 2009, Century 21 decided to shift their entire television advertising budget to online marketing. One of the things they did on their website was take the well-established MLS software that helps consumers find real estate listings and they made a smartphone application out of it. Suddenly anyone could download the app on their phone and search the MLS and find real estate inventory. Because it was tied directly to Century 21, this application was a successful component of their social media marketing campaign. What Century 21 has done is really smart. They understand social media currency and they are leveraging someone else's content (the MLS) to deliver value to their prospective clients.

Education is better than marketing

Your goal is to train your customers to buy from you, and to do that you need to give them the information necessary to make an informed buying decision. Think about the last time you made a purchase. You probably used the Internet to help you make that purchase and my guess is a handful of things occurred. You used a search engine like Google in the very beginning of the process. You also took mental or physical notes about all the features available to you, and you probably developed lists of your "must-haves" and "nice-to-haves." Once you had your buying criteria formulated, the next step was to figure out who you were going to buy from based on other factors such as convenience of location or shipping and price. Your customers are going through that very same process to make a purchase. If you give them information to educate and help them filter through their criteria you will train customers to buy from you.

Remember your niche

If you recall, this is one of the rules of engagement. What is that one attribute that makes your business a monopoly? What is it your customers cannot get from any other business? What is that *one thing* that represents your niche in your market? Once you know what that is – shout it from the rooftops! You'll discover the Internet is a really big world and there are plenty of potential customers out there who will resonate extremely well with your niche. They will come to you in droves and convert at a very high rate because you're speaking to them in their language.

Content for Your Marketing Funnel

Consumers of any product or service work through a process that starts with becoming aware of a need and ends with making a decision to purchase or not to purchase. At any moment in time you have potential customers considering your company within various stages of the decision process. They may be learning about you for the very first time, or comparing your products to another company's, or telling their boss/wife/coworker why they should or shouldn't buy from you. It's important to build content that communicates with these prospective customers no matter where they are in their decision journey with your company. To help you become intentional about creating content to satisfy customers at the different stages of decision making, here is what I call the Universal Marketing Funnel. Regardless of whether you are a B2B or B2C company, or whether you sell something complex or something commoditized, at some point your customer will work through these universal stages of the marketing funnel.

1. **Awareness:** This is the stage in which your potential customer becomes aware that your company exists. You need to create content your target audience will find interesting before they are in the market for what you sell. By creating this type of content you are exposing your business to potential customers while leading with value. For example, if you are a car dealer you might want to create blog articles or videos around how to winterize a vehicle or properly install a child seat, which will make a potential customer aware of your company. Pest control companies could create content about things homeowners can do on their own to fight off pesky insects. Accounting software companies could do a video series on ways to cut costs around the office. Thirty to forty percent of the content you create should be for the purposes of awareness and for exposing your knowledge to your target market.

2. **Evaluation:** This is the stage in which your customer is in the market for what you are selling and they are trying to formulate their buying criteria to understand and evaluate

all the features available to them, from you and your competitors. When I take my family to the beach, I want to look at all of the potential places to stay in correlation to the beach, restaurants, and other fun activities. If I'm planning to take my family on a beach vacation in Florida, I would love to read/ watch content about things to do in various beach towns, or the best beaches to watch the sunset, or what locations are best to see dolphins swimming offshore.

For a car dealer, an evaluation piece might be the pros and cons of hybrid versus gas-powered engines, or the pros and cons of SUVs versus minivans. For an accounting software company, an evaluation piece could be the pros and cons of cloud-based solutions versus desktop software. Like the awareness stage, 30% to 40% of your content should be about helping the customer evaluate your offering.

3. **Decision:** Now that your potential customers know what they want, they have to make a decision about where to buy it. They are asking themselves, "Why should I buy from you?" Here's your opportunity to strut your stuff and tell

stories about how much value you've delivered to others who have enjoyed your product or service. Whatever your niche is, maximize it by creating content around it so your customer can see why they should buy from you. Decision-based content should represent 20% but no more than 30% of your content. Too much horn tooting will turn off customers who are in the awareness or evaluation stage.

My experience has been that most business owners want to create lots of decision stage content and I have to spend a lot of time helping them see the value of creating content for the other stages. The biggest reason for building content within all three stages is that by doing so you are exposing your business to a much bigger target audience. In the funnel graphic, the Decision stage is smaller than the others. This means a company could be missing out on 60% to 80% of the potential customers they could engage with in social media. Additionally, customers who find you when they are in the decision stage are pretty set in what they want. You won't have much opportunity to sway them toward your features and benefits, which means unless you line up perfectly with their buying criteria you won't make the sale. However, if they find you earlier in the process then you have the opportunity to educate them on why the features and benefits you offer are a perfect fit for them.

For a lot of businesses, coming up with remarkable content can be challenging. That's why you should start with your key phrase spreadsheet and then refer to the 50 headline ideas provided in the Appendix section of this book to come up with great topics. Once you have great topics, consider these examples of remarkable content to build out your content strategy. Remember, the goal is to create content that people with read and share.

EXAMPLES OF EFFECTIVE CONTENT

Blog posts and Videos – Short blog posts (200-400 words) and 1-2 minute videos appeal to our on-demand, short-attention-span society.

Stories – Stories sell and are much better than feature dumps, however, don't just tell a story for the sake of sharing an experience. Make sure you can demonstrate how your company improved the life of an individual or helped another business save money or make money. That will be much more effective.

Product comparisons – Take your top products and stack them up in an unbiased way against the top three or four competitors in your market in a comparison matrix,. People like to quickly scan that type of information and share it with their followers. It's important to keep it unbiased. Don't compare the best features of your products against the worst features of your competitor's weakest products. People will see right through that. Not only will your reputation take a big hit, but your content will not be shared with their friends.

Product demos – Video demonstrations of how to install/attach/wear or use/enjoy a product are usually very successful. My 18-year-old son collects swords. He even has a website where he buys and reviews swords. He loves watching videos produced by manufacturers that show their swords chopping through items like water bottles and bamboo.

Lists of any kind – We've already established that most people have a very short attention span when it comes to the Internet, so when you can, avoid the 1,000-word monologue about a particular topic and take the time to organize your content with an easy-to-scan list, perhaps the "Top Ten Reasons to …" or " Five things to avoid when …" This format is widely consumed and shared.

Controversial opinion or counterpoint – Find those opportunities to flip users' perspectives upside down by attacking part of your industry with a controversial opinion or counterpoint that lines up nicely with your unique selling proposition. You'll be surprised at how much traffic you get with this type of content. Not only are you showing your industry knowledge from a unique perspective, but you are also making your audience aware of your niche.

Solicit feedback and responses – Finish your content pieces with open-ended questions or by asking people for their opinion. Encourage dialogue and spark conversation. When you create remarkable content and ask for feedback, you will get responses because your content is worthy of a remark.

Remember the tipping point in social media is getting other people to talk about you and share your content. The more interesting your content, the more likely your followers will share it with their followers and your community will grow exponentially. You literally need to create remarkable content that will grab the reader's attention and get them thinking about all the people they know who would be interested in it. Think about it this way. Did you drive by this building this morning on your way to work?

You probably have no idea because you've seen a thousand buildings in your city just like this one. Now take a look at this second photo.

Did you drive by this building this morning? Instantly you know you didn't. Why? This building is unique and memorable. By the way, that's a real building, no Photoshop software was used to create this picture. It is the Longaberger Baskets headquarters in Newark, Ohio. If you did find yourself driving by this building for the first time, would you tell someone? Would you take a photo with your smartphone and upload it to Facebook? Many people would.

When you are creating content for social media I want you to think about Longaberger Baskets headquarters and ask yourself how you can create remarkable content. By determining your social media currency, leading with value, and developing content within each stage of the Universal Marketing Funnel, you'll be in a good position to create unique and memorable content.

Social Rules - Developing Content:

Rule #23: Use your key phrase research to develop a content plan that is in alignment with what your customers want and need.

Rule #24: Create content around each stage of the Universal Marketing Funnel; Awareness, Evaluation, and Decision.

Rule #25: Find existing, archived knowledge that can be repurposed into blog articles or posts to share with followers and friends.

Rule #26: Create remarkable content that people want to share with their followers.

Rule #27: Build content around your niche and your unique selling proposition.

Rule #28: Periodically write something controversial to spur dialogue.

Rule #29: Ask open-ended questions and solicit feedback from your audience.

11. CONVERSION

I met my wife in the summer of 1989. I was a call center manager running the evening shift at a telemarketing company; she was a recent college grad looking for some part-time income until she found a real job. I used to run this cheesy ad in The Dallas Morning News that had a picture of a big hand holding a telephone [broadcasting]. I was always looking to add good people to the team [building community]. The moment she came in for her interview, I was hooked. That same day, I told a good friend (who would ultimately be the best man at our wedding) that I had just met my future wife. She worked there for a couple of months before I had an opportunity to talk with her in a social setting. The first time was when she needed a ride to pick up her car that had been getting serviced [leading with value]. The second time was a couple of weeks later when I overheard [listening] that most of the office was going out for drinks after the shift was over. This was when I had an opportunity to talk with her about things other than work and we discovered we had a lot of common interests [remarkable content]. Later that evening I asked her out on a date [call to action]. A few months later, I asked her to marry me and she said yes [conversion].

I know what you might be thinking, "this guy had the Tactical Wheel and the Universal Marketing Funnel in the back of his mind while he courted his wife." Not really, but I did know how to approach her in a way that could lead to a positive end result for both of us. Imagine what she would have said to me the first day we met if I walked up to her and said that I wanted to marry her? She would have run for the hills! Instead, she has been my wife for more than 20 years.

The ultimate goal of any marketing strategy is to convert visitors into buyers. Social media marketing is no different. Listening, building community, broadcasting, and producing remarkable content have all been steps in a process to get us to conversion. Remember, the litmus test for whether or not you have earned the right for conversion is if your prospects can engage in your social media content (i.e. read your blog, watch a video, etc.) and feel like that was a good use of their time. Then you've earned the right to ask people to take the next step or engage with you at a deeper level. If all you do is run around asking everybody you meet to get married, you'll turn off your prospects and they too will run for the hills.

Now Buyers and Future Buyers

There are two types of buyers when it comes to social media and Internet marketing in general. One is what I call the *now buyer* and the other is the *future buyer*. The now buyer is someone who has a burning need they're trying to satisfy, they have a budget and a time frame. The future buyer is someone who has a dream or is living with a problem, but they're not yet motivated to solve it; yet they're still out there just trying to understand what's available to them.

It's important to understand these two different types of buyers because they're both willing to engage with you via social media, but they'll respond in different ways for different reasons. The image below shows that only about 10% to 15% of the leads you generate will be now buyer leads or what we call sales-ready leads. About 70% to 80% of the leads generated through social media will be future buyers; people who are not sales-ready but are still interested in learning about a product or service.

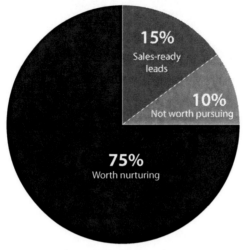

Source: Marketing Sherpa 2008

I encourage you to think about future buyers as your ideal candidates for conversion through social media. We love to get the now buyers because they're ready to buy and they have an open checkbook and a need, but it's a small percentage of the people who are engaging with you in social media. If you build your conversion activities only around the now buyer, you'll be limited in the amount of leads you create and sales you make through social media.

Types of Calls to Action

You also need to understand the different types of calls to action: active and passive. Active calls to action are those in which you are clearly communicating to the potential customer what their next step is and the benefits to them for taking it. Passive calls to action are when you are making sure that when someone is ready to take the next step you have given them an avenue to do that. A very common example of a passive call to action is to make sure your phone number is clearly visible on every bit of your social media content.

Effective social media strategies use both types of call to action, depending on the platform and type of content being produced. For example, if you are posting an awareness blog, then having an active call to action would not be appropriate; however, you could certainly make sure your phone number is visible in the top right corner of the masthead. On the other hand, if someone is looking for a place to eat, like in the Park Lane example I mentioned earlier, it's fine to jump in with an active call to action and offer a coupon for free garlic fries.

I will get into this in more detail within the different platform chapters, but it is important to include a graphic of your contact information in any and all social media account backgrounds or logos. If someone lands on your Facebook page or your Twitter account, they should very quickly find your phone number and your website.

Fair Exchange of Value

The fuel for maximizing any conversion is making sure you have a fair exchange of value. What the user is getting in return for their action is greater than the effort or cost to them. What that basically means is you're getting something valuable from them, their engagement, their contact information or their order; in return you have to give them something they deem valuable.

This could be as simple as liking your Facebook page. The user will have to believe what they receive as a result of liking your page is greater than the effort of clicking the Like button and the cost of having to see your posts on their News Feed. It could also be as complicated as registering to attend a webinar or workshop you're hosting. To maximize conversions, the user will need to be convinced the information you require them to provide and the time they have to invest in attending the event are less than the value they will receive as a result of their efforts. If you want to generate leads, you need to cross that threshold of fair exchange of value. Why would they take the next step? Remember WIIFM – What's In It For Me? Maybe they are giving you their email address in your opt-in or subscriber form to get a white paper, or a personalized evaluation, or to download a smartphone application. They have to perceive the value they are getting is greater than what they are giving.

The following example shows a Splash Media client who is using a blog article to generate leads. The article itself is at the evaluation stage of the funnel we covered in the previous chapter therefore it is okay to have an active call to action within the post. The offer is for a 30-day free trial of a software solution. The client generates a lot of highly qualified leads because the call to action is relevant with the topic being discussed. There is fair exchange of value because the lead is getting access to the software for free to determine if it will be helpful to them before making a purchase.

Here is an example of an active call to action inside a blog to drive leads for 30-day free trial.

Once you figure out what it will take to get them to take the next step, you have to sell it. Just having a link to an offer isn't enough. You have to promote the opportunity for them to take the next step. What I've discovered is that most companies tend to fall into two camps when it comes to web conversion:

They try too hard to sell the product or service they offer. This is a problem because most customers need to talk with a salesperson at some point. Your web presence will rarely do an adequate job selling what you do. Your true intention is to generate a lead for a salesperson. It's your salesperson's job to make the sale; what you are doing online is selling the conversion.

They are too passive because they believe a call to action will somehow turn off their customers. This is just silly. If you have a fair exchange of value then your prospective customers will never think giving information to get value is a turnoff.

Remember Your ABCs = Always Be Closing

You want to be intentional about getting people to engage when they're ready, which means you don't create a blog or other piece of content without the ABCs. You have to always think about how you can to give somebody the opportunity to take the next step.

Think about these questions for a minute. Who are your users? Who are these people who will be engaging with your social media content and finding this content fascinating and remarkable? What are their motives? What is it they're hoping to accomplish by being a part of your community or reading your material? I'm guessing their motives are not to help you grow your email list. I'm guessing it's not to have your sales rep call them and try to sell them something. These are not their motives. They're probably more interested in getting what they want, impressing their friends/spouse/boss, keeping their job, getting promoted, or increasing their knowledge. Maybe they're motivated to bring in more business for their company, which will put more money in their pocket. Perhaps they are like most people and they would prefer to read or watch a piece of content to get the information they need, rather than get it from another person in a sales presentation or sales call. Remember, people love to buy but hate to be sold.

Take a step back and think about who your users are as human beings with real needs, not just numbers in your web stats. When you consider the real people and their real needs you can then understand what is motivating them and give them an opportunity to engage with you in a meaningful way that satisfies their motives. Social media allows you to generate productive conversations in a style that appeals to your user.

Here is a B2C example from a jewelry store client of Splash Media's that ties all of this together. They understand their customer; mainly women. In this example, our client understands their customers' motives; women who want to give something to their man on Father's Day. They understand fair exchange of value; they are making it extremely easy to enter to win a very expensive watch. Samuels Jewelers was able to leverage all of this into a campaign that helped them build community. The result was huge growth in their Twitter community, which was the goal, but also huge growth in their Facebook community as people started telling others about the special offer.

Here is a B2C example of using an active call to action inside Facebook to build community on Twitter.

Here are examples of effective calls to action that we have used for our clients to generate conversions through social media.

EXAMPLES OF EFFECTIVE CALLS TO ACTION

Request a quote or a catalog – This may sound simple, but here's a good example of how it can work for you. Splash Media has a whirlpool bathtub client who happens to sell whirlpool tubs that cost about four times more than the market leader. No one I know will add a $4000 whirlpool bathtub to a website shopping cart and check out online. The company's number one goal is for potential customers to engage with them via social media and then request their beautiful catalog that tells exactly why their products are worth every penny.

Educational event – Remember, your potential customers are trying to make informed decisions; therefore, putting on events like webinars or workshops can be an effective way to get them to take the next step. One of my clients hosts a webinar every Tuesday and Thursday at 10:00 a.m. They promote it online and have a registration form for the event. During the webinar, the CEO gives a 10-slide PowerPoint presentation that provides an overview of their solution and then opens it up for questions. Some weeks they receive as many as 15-20 leads from the webinar; but if no one registers for a particular session, the CEO does something else with his time.

Special offers – Offering coupons, gift cards and discounts can be very effective for many businesses.

Free analysis - If you're a B2B or consulting company, you can offer a free analysis during which you gather data from your customers' environment, conduct research and put together a specialized report for their team. Splash Media does that on our website and we get a 5% to 10% conversion rate through social media with the free analysis we offer.

Promotional products – Many businesses have experienced surprising results by offering something as simple as a baseball cap with their company logo on it.

Buyer's kit - If your industry consists of long sales cycles and sales-by-committee, offering buyer's kits are a great way to generate leads by sending anyone who opts-in information that will educate them on the process and help them internally promote a change within their organization.

Technical resource area – This is a spot on your website and social media environments where you have a lot of good technical data that your potential buyers need, but you lock it up in a library where they have to opt-in to gain access to it.

Smart phone applications – You could do something like the Century 21 example I mentioned earlier, where they integrated MLS into an application for their target market.

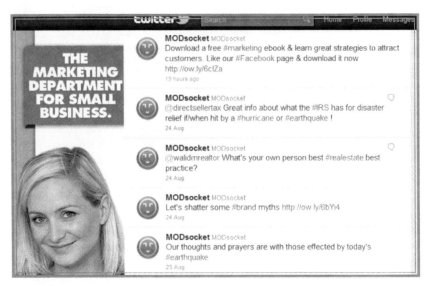

Using the 90/10 rule, ModSocket promotes a free offer in Twitter for users to try their online marketing system.

Social Rules - Conversion:

Rule #30: Integrate passive calls to action that are clearly visible on every page of your website and social media platforms.

Rule #31: Use active calls to action within the copy of evaluation and decision blog posts, encouraging users to take the next step.

Rule #32: Develop something useful for future buyers that can be given away if they opt-in by providing contact information.

Rule #33: Remember fair exchange of value and only ask for information you need to fulfill their request.

Rule #34: Don't treat future buyers and now buyers the same. Send now buyers to your sales team and put future buyers into a lead-nurturing process.

Part 3

SOCIAL MEDIA PLATFORMS

12. FACEBOOK

Think about the first time you heard about this new website called Facebook. Someone, probably a teenager, told you it was a really cool site that allows you to connect with your friends so you can keep them up to date regarding your life. If you were like me, you probably thought "What a waste of time!" Yes, I must admit, the first time I heard about Facebook, I never expected it to be what it has become, and I'm in the business. No wonder it has been hard for entrepreneurs and business owners to get a handle on Facebook's importance. Now, here you are with this book in your hands. My guess is that one of the main reasons you are reading this book is to figure out how Facebook can help you grow your business.

Before I jump right into Facebook, I'd like to dispel a myth that I'm sure a lot of business owners have when they think about using Facebook as a marketing tool. The biggest myth is Facebook is only about individuals talking about where they went to high school, what they did today, and what they did on vacation with no relevance to the average business person. There is an element of voyeurism on Facebook that makes it popular because people are interested in looking at photos and updates from family and friends. Facebook is revolutionizing the way we communicate and connect. This is the element that fuels the fire and keeps people coming back to Facebook.

I mentioned earlier that I've had the opportunity to speak all over the country on social media through our Social Media for CEOs Boot Camps, and although I love it and am passionate about it, my speaking engagements cause me to be on the road quite a bit. I remember one day landing in Austin, Texas, and getting to my hotel room the night before a boot camp and logging on to Facebook to discover my 15-year-old son had a new girlfriend. This was his first girlfriend, and the way I found out was he changed his Facebook status from *Single* to *In a Relationship*. Of course I posted a message to him on his wall congratulating him and letting him know it was inevitable that this story would make it to my onstage presentation. What was funny to me was he actually clicked Like on the wall post. Sometimes it can be easier to communicate online than through any other medium, especially for a teenage boy with his dad.

The myth, however, is that this type of behavior is the only thing going on. For businesses, Facebook is a built-in endorsement and testimonial machine. Why do companies pay big bucks for famous people to endorse their products and some businesses love to show testimonials of customers who have used their products or services? The answer is obvious; endorsements and testimonials help companies transfer trust to the potential customer. "If Michael Jordan says it's good, then it must be good." Imagine a world where you were able to create trust transference on a grand scale, but instead of the endorser being a celebrity or some stranger who has used your product, it's a prospect's Mom, Dad, the best man at their wedding, or the pastor of their church. That's the power of Facebook for business. If you don't believe me, watch commercials tonight on TV. Notice how many of the big brands are encouraging you to visit their Facebook page. The big brands get it.

Facebook is absolutely important for business because it's truly becoming the 800-pound gorilla in social media. It's a way you'll connect with your customers, prospects, partners, employees, potential employees and influencers. It's a place where you'll be able to offer advice, share knowledge and help others. It's also a place to generate leads and sales—if you do it the right way.

The core idea behind Facebook is people sharing information and media with their friends, family and coworkers. Facebook is quickly becoming the Internet inside the Internet. What makes the Internet great is it provides access to anything and everything. But, on the other side of the coin, what makes the Internet challenging is it provides access to anything and everything. This has been a big problem with the wide-spread adoption of the Internet over the past 15 years. There have been many attempts to help organize this information in a useful way for the common Internet user.

One of the first ways that is still very prevalent today, is to leverage search engines using artificial intelligence, commonly known as spiders or crawlers, to read Internet content to determine relevance and importance and provide the visitor of a search engine with useful information based on key phrases they typed into the search field. But now, as a result of Facebook and social media, we're starting to see the shift to what I call *social search*, which is tapping into the advice and opinions of people we trust to find Internet content that is relevant rather than letting search engine crawlers tell us what is important. This is also known as word-of-mouth advertising on steroids, and I think this ultimately begins at Facebook. Because of its sheer size Facebook provides a platform for us to discover what content we can trust. For instance, if someone you know and trust says they finally got rid of those pesky termites because they used XYZ Company, you'll be more likely trust this company when you have a similar pest problem.

Another interesting element Facebook provides that is better than traditional search engines is the ability for people to share unstructured content. For instance, search engines are good at providing relevant structured content (web page, press release, blog, etc.) but what's great about social media is your trusted friends are posting all different types of content you might find relevant. They may share vacation photos and their experience at a particular hotel or restaurant you may want to check out. They're creating access to information that isn't easily accessible in any other format. They're also acting as an unofficial endorser because this information is coming from people you know and trust.

Recently I was having lunch with dear friends Ajit and Sara, who were passing through Dallas on their way to Brazil. Ajit was so impressed with the wine list of this tiny hole-in-the-wall restaurant my wife had picked that he took a picture of the wine list and posted it on Facebook with an endorsement recommending to anyone who had a scheduled layover in Dallas to check out the restaurant. Ajit is a world traveler and known as a wine connoisseur. He also has over 900 friends on Facebook. Content like this would never make it to a search engine, but you can imagine the impact it made for this small business. Imagine the power behind that kind of endorsement for your business.

> **Facebook Statistics**
> - More than 750 million users.
> - 136 million visitors every single day in the United States.
> - 46 years (400,000 hours) of YouTube videos are watched on Facebook every day.
> - 50% of Facebook users make more than $60,000 annually.*
> - 32% of people with Facebook profiles make over $100,000 annually.*
> - 74 % of Facebook users are over the age of 18.*
> - The average user has more than 130 Facebook friends.*
>
> *According to Quantcast*

When you think about the 750 million people on Facebook primarily over the age of 18 who make more than $60,000 a year, you can be confident your customers, prospects and potential employees are on Facebook. Why not take advantage of this great opportunity to engage, connect and share useful information with them.

Purpose of Facebook for Businesses

Facebook is primarily a broadcast site, so your focus will be in building and nurturing a community and promoting content to your community so they will eventually make it to your website or blog.

- **Build awareness about your brand in the community.** By sharing your expertise with others you add value and build credibility and visibility. When your community starts engaging with your Facebook page, their friends will become aware of your business because their activity on your page will show up on their friends' News Feed.

- **Provide customer service.** Your customers will use your Facebook page as a customer service tool. Customers do not want to come to your website as much anymore to deal with customer service issues or call your toll-free number and wait on the phone for 20 minutes to deal with customer service issues. Instead, they'll post customer service issues where they are, and they'll expect you to respond and deal with them online.

- **Place and promote content on followers' news pages, which is much more effective than email marketing.** When your followers log into Facebook, they'll see content you've posted on your page. In the follow graphic, you can see updates from companies I follow as well as updates from my friends. Most of us delete emails in our inboxes that aren't extremely relevant. In contrast, Facebook claims that of their 750 million plus users, 50% log in at least once per day. Having your message appear on the News Feed of your followers gives you a much better chance to have your message read.

- **Share your knowledge.** Promote your blogs, news and events through Facebook. Here's a quick tour of a company page. Your Facebook environment offers many opportunities to deliver information to your followers that will keep them engaged and coming back for more.

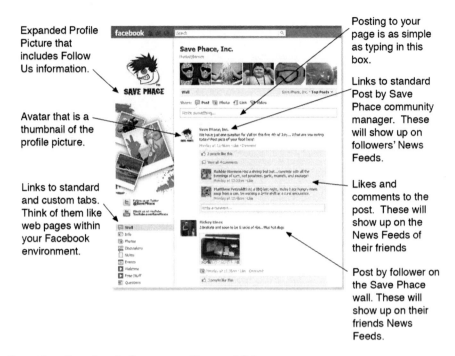

Creating Facebook Company Pages 101

For setting up accounts in Facebook and all the other social media sites we will discuss in Part 3, there are "How To" videos available for you in the resource section of the Splash Media website. Visit www.splashmedia.com/resources to access those videos and the many other resources presented in this book.

Profiles are for people and Pages are for businesses. You must have a Facebook account to create a company page. *Personal accounts are not your business page.* If you have friends, even if it looks like a company page, you do not have a company page, because you can "like" a company page but you cannot "friend" a company page.

Multiple Pages vs. One Page: There's no limit to the number of pages you can set up, so you might consider having one page for your company and then separate pages for the different products or services you provide. There are pros and cons to each. For a small business, I'm a fan of having one company page. If you're an enterprise business, you might consider breaking it up by division or by different product segments.

As a small business owner, you'll want to have one company page because community building for companies is not an easy thing to do on Facebook. Therefore, the more pages you have the more effort it will take to build effective community for your business because you've now spread it across multiple pages on Facebook.

Multiple Administrators: You can have and assign an unlimited number of administrators for your page, which I strongly recommend. You don't want to be the only administrator of your page.

Unlimited Likes (Fans): There is no limit to the number of fans or "likes" you can have on a company page. On a personal profile page you are limited to 5,000 friends.

Post on other pages: As a company you can write wall posts on other company's pages, which enables you to promote your business to other business communities.

Securing Custom URL: There's a land grab going on over at Facebook and it's really important to set up a company page, get your 25 "likes," and claim the real estate, www.facebook.com/yourcompanyname. This will be just as important to your business in a couple of years or less than it was to have a website address that was www.yourcompanyname.com in the '90's. After you set up your company page, go to www.facebook.com/username. There you will be able to check the availability and claim your username. Once it is selected, you won't be able to change it or transfer ownership to another party, so make sure you pick a name that most closely represents your company name.

The Tactical Wheel on Facebook

Listening

Listening in Facebook is not as easy as it is on other platforms. Google has a hard time crawling Facebook status updates and providing you with useful information from Google alerts. In order to look for posts and people of interest, follow this three-step process using the search function on Facebook. This will help you find people and other businesses who are interested in the same topics who could be influencers and potential customers.

Step 1: Type in key phrase with quotes and click on "See more results".

Step 2: Find pages to like and groups to join.

Step 3: Click on "Posts by Everyone" to find influencers talking about the key phrase.

Another way of listening is by paying attention to the comments being posted on your page, and then responding to those appropriately. Make sure you have systems in place for checking wall posts frequently and responding appropriately in timely fashion. You can set up Facebook to send you an email whenever anyone posts on your page.

Building Community on Facebook

For most businesses, your initial goal should be to get 500 or more "likes" or fans of your page. In most cases, once your community grows to about 500 fans, you have reached a tipping point with regard to engagement. Here are some ideas to get you there as quickly as possible.

Welcome Tab/Page: Also known as fangating, you'll want to create a custom Welcome tab on your company page that acts as a landing page for any new visitors. Anyone who accesses your page and has not yet "liked" it will be automatically directed to your welcome page, which should have a brief description of what to expect by liking your page, what your company is all about and perhaps a quick video or a promotional item for becoming a new fan. Be sure to include a large call-to-action arrow directing people to like your page at the top of the screen. People who have already liked your page will not see the welcome message again unless they click on it from the left-hand navigational bar.

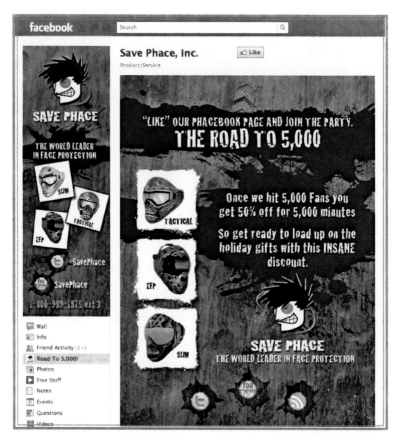

Welcome tab that encourages users to like your page. It also includes clickable icons to other social media environments.

Customized Tabs: To enhance a user's experience you can create customized tabs that will incorporate other social media content right into your Facebook environment. At Splash Media, we use ShortStack.com to set these up for our clients. They offer tools to set up custom tabs that range in price from free to a few hundred dollars per month. In the following example, you can see we have added direct access to our client's YouTube and Twitter environments. Because they are a well-respected B2C retailer, we have also included a review tab so customers can write review about their experiences.

Custom tabs give you the ability to incorporate other social media environments.

Encourage engagement: As you're posting content on your Facebook company page, ask open-ended questions and encourage people to talk. Every time someone posts or comments on your page, whether it's answering a question you asked or just writing on your wall, a post will show up on their wall which will give you visibility to all of their friends. Considering the average Facebook user has more than 130 friends, visitor wall posts can have a significant effect on your exposure rate.

Get ranked: EdgeRank is the system Facebook uses to calculate which posts make it into the "Top Stories" part of the News Feed.

It is essential to get your Status Updates into the Top Stories feed, otherwise your post will lose its momentum in as little as 24 hours. Pages get EdgeRanked based on how actively Fans interact with the page content; the more interactions, the higher the ranking. Types of interactions include users sharing, commenting, and liking your posts.

Facebook ads: Leveraging Facebook ads in the beginning of your social media marketing plan will help you get to your critical mass of 500 plus fans quickly. Your Facebook ad should be tied to a custom Facebook Welcome Tab and a special offer or promotion.

Let's walk through how to create ads that will quickly build your community.

CREATING YOUR FACEBOOK AD

- Click on "Create an Ad" button on the top right of your page.
- Complete each step as the tutorial wizard describes.
- Design your ad.
- Determine your target: based on geography, demographic or your offering (the better your target, the more you'll connect to potential customers).
- Decide on a name for your ad.
- Determine your budget (expect to pay $1.00 - $1.50 for each new fan).
- Uncheck the "Run Campaign Continuously."
- Deactivate the end date of your campaign.
- Choose pay-per-click (PPC) rather than cost-per-thousand (CPM) – With CPM you are charged for anyone who sees the ad, rather than clicks.
- Determine your maximum bid (it's best to start off in the middle-high bid range).

Remember to create your ad with two key elements: Call to Action and Key Phrases. The idea behind the ad is to get people to click on it, so use action words like "visit page," "get it now," "sign up today," or "download free e-book," etc. Refer back to your keywords and key phrases list to choose the words that resonate well with your target audience.

After you've reviewed your ad and you're happy with the targeting you've selected, go ahead and place the order. You'll hear back from Facebook within approximately 24 hours that your ad has been approved. Take a screenshot of your ad and save it for your records. You'll want to come back to that when you're through running the campaign and make notes on the effectiveness of that ad based on how many "likes" you received relative to how much money you spent on the ad. Also, in the beginning of your ad campaign, check your ad daily. If you're not getting any "likes' or you're paying more than $1.50 per "like," consider making adjustments to the ad.

Building Community Off Facebook

In addition to everything you do on Facebook, there are valuable ways to build community for your Facebook page in other environments.

Add "Like" Button Everywhere: One of the most important things you can do is add the "Like" button to your website and blog. This makes it extremely easy for someone with a Facebook profile to simply click the button and "like" your page. Facebook has a free plug-in you can download and install onto your website and blog page. You can also add a "Connect on Facebook" message in your newsletter and email signatures. Each time someone "likes" your page, that announcement will show up on their profile wall which exposes you to all of their friends.

Send an Email Announcement: Let your customers and prospects know you're now on Facebook and share what they can expect from liking your page. Explain to them the advantages they'll receive, such as special promotions, updates about new products and access to Facebook-only events.

Broadcasting

As you may remember, the broadcasting stage of your social media marketing campaign is all about posting value-added information to your target audience. Simply engaging with your community on Facebook is also broadcasting. Every business, whether you're B2B or B2C, should post a minimum of three to four times per week. If you are a B2C company that's open seven days a week, I would encourage you to post every day of the week.

Use "@" tag to promote and give visibility to others: If you're talking about another company that has a Facebook page, you can use the "@"sign in front of their Facebook profile name and it will add a direct link to that company's page as well as show up on their wall. Tagging other pages is a great way to generate conversations with key influencers on Facebook.

Ask Open-Ended Questions: Get people dialoguing and talking about or responding to your posts. This is really important because it will help your content go viral. When someone comments on your page their activity will show up on their News Feed which is seen by all of their friends on Facebook which, in turn, gives you more visibility to potential customers.

Use good thumbnail photos: When adding external links in your Facebook status update make sure you select the best thumbnail photo from the linked page to post.

Be sure to select photos that inspire engagement.

Because you cannot tag others in photos, ask visitors of the page to tag themselves on photos you upload. The following example is of a car dealer who takes pictures of customers with their new car and post the picture to Facebook. The customer can go onto their page and tag themselves in the picture. By doing so, the picture will also show up on the customer's friends' News Feed.

Be the Last to Comment: When your comment is the last one in a comment thread of your own wall, the people who shared comments will get a notification that you responded. This is important because it demonstrates you're listening and engaged.

Send private updates: You can create a direct message or private update to go to all of your fans or a subset of your fan base. This is a great way to promote special offers. Simply log in as the administrator of your page and click the "Edit Page" in the upper right side of the Facebook business page. On the left navigation bar, click the "Resources" button and then select "Send an Update." You'll be able to target specific demographics such as location, age or sex of the people who have "liked" your page. You can even attach links or videos. If you want to create a community within a community, or a special promotion to a subset, this is a great way to do it. You'll find you get much better results by doing this with your followers or "likes" on Facebook than even email marketing today.

Promote your blog headline as a post. We'll talk more about his in the Blogging chapter, but for now you should use your keyword-rich headline as a wall post on your company page and add the link to the blog using a URL shortener, such as bit.ly, to track your click-through rate.

Post General Information: General statements relevant to your target audience get a lot of engagement. The more engagement, the more your company will show up in the News Feed of your friends who are connected to your fans, your followers or to your "likes." Here's an example that illustrates how a very simple statement resulted in a great deal of engagement (122 likes and 14 comments) for one of our Splash Media clients.

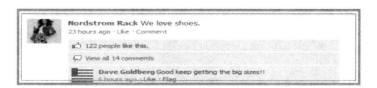

Developing Content

When I talk about content on Facebook what I'm really talking about is leveraging content that you've created at other places to gain exposure in Facebook.

Use Notes Feature for Blog Teaser: You can use the Notes feature on your Facebook page to build interest and drive traffic to a blog post by writing a one- or two-paragraph snippet of the blog. Within the note include a hyperlink that says "to read more about (targeted key phrase)" and provide the hyperlink over to the blog.

This is important because the Notes pages are currently the only section of Facebook that Google is indexing. I've seen this happen many times where a search engine optimized Facebook note will actually show up in the Google search results higher than a company's website.

Using Facebook Note to promote and tease blog articles. This note includes keyword-rich links back to the blog article.

Leverage Events: When you're adding events to the "events" tab, make sure to include a photo for the event with all the details and be very clear how people can register to attend. More than likely they'll not just indicate they're attending the event, which is one of the options in Facebook, but they'll be linked to another environment to register which might be your website, your blog or a registration service like Eventbrite.

Add Facebook Livestream: You can add Livestream to your Facebook page to deliver live video content to your fans via a webcam. Everything will be recorded and made available in an on-demand library. This takes webinars to the next level. Imagine promoting an informative webinar your target audience would find compelling, however they have to go to your Facebook page and "like" it before than can get access to the webinar.

Create Video Vault: I recommend you take at least three of your videos you have on YouTube and upload them into the Facebook vault so they'll always be available to new visitors.

Swap them out periodically to keep them fresh. At Splash Media, we have used videos as a tease to get people to "like" a client's page where the pre-like tab showed a grayed-out version of video content. Once the visitor clicked on the "Like" button they were able to access the video.

Conversion

There are two conversion goals on Facebook.

1. Encourage users to become a lead or purchase a product. At Splash Media, we've helped our clients do everything from sell cars, jewelry, face masks, and much more through Facebook. We've also generated leads for attorneys, LASIK doctors, software companies and then some. Don't be afraid to use this powerful platform to grow your business.

2. Encourage visitors to "like" your page. By earning new "likes" you have a direct link to potential customers. You'll benefit from exposure to their friends based on their comments, wall posts and profile. You'll also be able to communicate with them in a format more visible than your traditional email database.

Strategies for Conversion

1. **Facebook promotions:** There are many different types of promotions within Facebook that are designed to build community for both B2C and B2C companies. Here are some examples:

   - **Road to 2000 fans** – Give away more and more valuable prizes as you reach predetermined milestones of "likes." For example, you might randomly give away a $100 gift card once you have 500 fans, then give away a $300 gift card (or iPad, TV, etc.) at 1000 fans and so on.

   - **Premium content** – If a user likes your page, give them access to premium content such as an e-book, exclusive video, or a free analysis.

   - **Competition** – Have users upload pictures of themselves using your product or your company logo, then have them get as many people as possible to comment on their photo (by default, their friends won't be able to comment unless they first "like" your page). The user with the most "likes" after a certain time wins a prize. Prizes could be your sponsorship of their Little League team, a month of free services, a free product, etc.

Special note: All Facebook conditions can be accessed by clicking on the Terms link at the bottom of your Facebook page. For promotional guidelines go to: https://www.facebook.com/promotions_guidelines.php

2. **Monthly Awareness Campaign**

Each month create one campaign that's centered on building awareness for one of your products or services. As you're creating content of interest for your target audience they will be "liking" your posts or adding to the conversation with their comments, which will allow you to become exposed to their friends.

For example, let's say you're a company that's in the business of organizing pantries, closets and garages. In the springtime, you might want to post content around spring-cleaning tips or how to organize your life. You should post different tips as status updates on your wall throughout the month, as well as linking to a blog about the same topic. Simultaneously you'll promote products that tie into the topic several times during the month. For example, you can offer a $50 off coupon to anyone who purchases a closet organization system valued at $200 or more.

With this type of awareness campaign you're providing relevant, useful information for people who are interested in your products and you're giving them an opportunity to purchase from you by using an offer or coupon.

You now know enough about Facebook to give your business a presence in the world's largest social network. Remember to start with a strategy and develop a purpose statement that connects the dots between this powerful medium and where you're trying to take your business. For smart marketers, Facebook can help you turn strangers into friends, friends into customers, and customers into evangelists, more than just about any other platform.

Social Rules - Facebook:

Rule #35: Facebook profiles are for people and pages are for companies. If your company Facebook presence has friends, then it is not set up correctly.

Rule #36: Secure a custom URL. Set up Facebook ads to jump start your community. Getting to 500 fans tends to be the tipping point for most company pages.

Rule #37: Listen within Facebook by searching "posts by everyone" using key phrases and by paying attention to comments being posted on your page.

Rule #38: Build community on Facebook by integrating a custom welcome tab, encouraging engagement with open-ended questions, offering promotions and placing ads.

Rule #39: Build community off Facebook by adding the "Like" button to all of your online and offline collateral.

Rule #40: Within Broadcasting, use the @tag to give visibility to others, send private updates, create monthly awareness campaigns and promote your blog posts.

Rule #41: It is easy to develop content on Facebook by using the notes option to create a blog teaser and uploading videos to your video vault.

13. TWITTER

What is Twitter and why should I care?

Sound familiar? I get asked this question all of the time at our Social Media for CEOs Boot Camps, and I know exactly where you're coming from. We hear about how celebrities are sharing what they're doing and where they're eating, but what about a business owner? What's in it for you?

Twitter is just like any other social media environment. It's a place to find people to connect with in your journey to turn friends into customers and customers into evangelists. You'll be happy to know you can build an amazing community that's engaged and responsive to you without having to share what you had for dinner last night or that you're aching from a screaming hangover. Because so many people are talking on Twitter—it's the most open platform (all you have to do is butt into a conversation that's already happening)—you'll find Twitter to be perfect for listening and learning what your target audience cares about. Forget focus groups. Twitter enables you to tap into the real-time thoughts and opinions of your customers. Because so many users on Twitter share their issues and problems, it's also an excellent place to harvest prospects by jumping in to help prospective customers solve their problems.

Benefits of Twitter for Your Business

High Traffic: Twitter is the seventh-most-visited website on the Internet in the United States, according to Alexa. Twitter receives more than 90 million unique visitors every single day, and that number is growing by leaps and bounds month after month. The following chart from Quantcast, shows the incredible traffic growth that they've received, making Twitter an important pond for you to fish in. However, most people access twitter from other devices, such as their mobile phones, so the actual number of people who interact with Twitter on a daily basis is staggering.

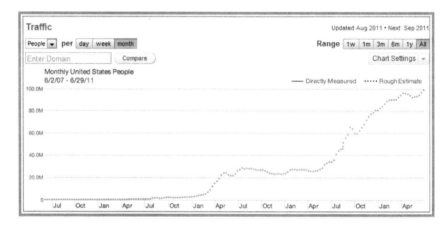

Efficient Micro-blogging: Twitter is a micro-blogging site where you add value and have conversations using messages that are 140 characters or less. Because of the character count limit, Twitter has become a very popular platform because it forces people to think and write with concise and crisp communication. It's a bit like text messaging in both its brevity and its popularity. Just like texting, Twitter is popular for a couple of reasons. First, the short messages make it appealing because it can be delivered and retrieved faster than voicemail messages and emails. The other reason for its popularity is it can be accessed from just about any mobile device, often without requiring a Wi-Fi network. This means you'll be able to participate in conversations quickly, as they happen, so you can easily expose your brand and influence decisions—but you have to move fast. The shelf life of a conversation on Twitter is literally mere seconds.

Effective Broadcast Site: As you will see in the Blog chapter, social media sites like Twitter are considered broadcast sites to help drive traffic to your website and blog. The primary purpose of leveraging your visibility on Twitter is to engage in conversation and draw people to other environments where you can add more value.

Powerful Search Engine: Twitter is also a very powerful search engine that will give you insight into the social media conversation. Just as Google is a search engine that provides relevant information on a particular topic or subject when you do a search, Twitter has that same capability. The big difference between Twitter and Google is Twitter's search results are in real time.

For example, at the time of this writing, Japan's earthquake and tsunami happened just a few months ago. If you did a search for Japan on Twitter, 90% of what showed up on the first page was related to the devastation of the earthquake and its impact on the people of Japan. But if you do a search for Japan in Google, the results would be pretty much what you would see today, only 10% to 20% of the results on the first page of Google would be about the tsunami. All the other results would be related to the history of Japan, news related to the economy of Japan, and various other sites, such as Wikipedia. While this content is relevant, it's not as real-time as what you receive by doing a search on Twitter. Earlier, I shared the story about finding out about Osama bin Laden's death via Twitter before the news broke on the local news or the President's press conference. I guarantee you, if I had gone to

Google instead of Twitter that evening I wouldn't have found out about the breaking news of bin Laden's death.

Wide Demographic: According to Quantcast, 83% of Twitter users are age 18 or older, and the majority of those are over the age of 30. Other than LinkedIn, Twitter provides access to the largest percentage of adults. If your target audience is between the ages of 25 to 54 years old, you need to be on Twitter

The Purpose of Twitter for Business

Platform for Listening: Twitter is a terrific place to listen to the social media conversation. You can view other people's content as well as watch conversations among different users and their reactions to current events. This helps you see what's on the mind of your target market and react quickly to their needs and interests.

Share Your Brand's Personality: Of all the different social media environments, Twitter is where you can really let your personality and company culture shine through. You may have heard Twitter described as the cocktail party of social media. In a very real way it is a platform that's lively and interactive with short dialogue occurring among acquaintances. Remember, people do business with people, which makes the personal interaction happening on Twitter in real time a valuable asset to any business.

A successful example of a company leveraging the people-doing-business-with-people concept is Zappos. Zappos CEO, Tony Hsieh (pronounced Shay), has been tweeting for a long time. If you follow him, you'll notice 90% of his tweets have nothing to do with selling shoes or pushing his agenda. The reason for this is he wants you to have a personal connection with his brand

and him so you'll remember Zappos when you consider making a shoe purchase.

Demonstrate knowledge and expertise: Just like with your other social media platforms, Twitter is a forum for adding value by offering advice or instructions, as well as answering questions and getting your target market to view you as a thought leader within your industry.

Share Real-Time Updates: Twitter enables you to quickly update your followers, customers, and prospects about what's happening with you and your company. On a personal level, Twitter can be instrumental in quickly broadcasting updates to your entire network.

For example, I'm involved with a church in the Dallas area and on Thanksgiving of 2009 our pastor's world changed. Matt is in his early 30s, and on the morning of Thanksgiving he woke up like he does every day, went to grab some coffee and pat his little boy on the head when he suddenly started to have a seizure. The next thing he knew, he was waking up in the hospital and found out he had a tumor in his brain about the size of an egg that needed to be removed immediately. The surgery was scheduled Friday of the following week. The day before his surgery he shot a video that was uploaded to YouTube and the church's website because he had no idea what might be next for him. Would he come out of the surgery? Would he remember his family and church? Would he be able to speak? The surgery went incredibly well, but it was subsequently followed by months of chemotherapy and radiation. As you might imagine, the 5000-plus people who attend our church were greatly concerned about his well-being. They wanted to know how he was doing and at the same time wanted to respect his family's privacy during the recovery process. Twitter was the saving grace for all of us because it gave Matt and his family an opportunity to communicate in a broadcast medium about his progress without the process being a burden. In addition, Twitter allows anyone to go online and follow the update status of a user without waiting for a friend request to be approved (or being denied based on friend count limitations), which is the case on Facebook. It also allowed people from all over the world to stay up to date on his progress. I can't tell you how many times I ran into someone in my travels that asked me about Matt and told me they were following him on Twitter. Matt is fully recovered today, by the grace of God, and still on Twitter. You can follow him @MattChandler74.

Drive Traffic to Your Blog: Twitter is a great way to broadcast when you have new content to share. It allows you to create a compelling headline and attach a direct link to your blog or any individual page on your website. Not everyone who follows you would likely have signed up for your blog's RSS feed, but when they see content that interests them on Twitter they can easily click through to your blog. Think of Twitter as a busy highway, and your posts as exit ramps to your blog.

Capitalize on Lowest Barrier to Entry: Twitter is really one of the lowest barriers of entry to connect with others, as was the case with Matt. You can casually follow or un-follow someone without any formal invitation. You can also break through status barriers and connect directly with high-level executives and industry mavens, as I will explain later in this chapter.

The Power of the Hashtag (#)

Simply put, a hashtag is a word or a phrase that's connected to a pound sign (#) without any spaces in between (#socialmedia). The idea behind the hashtag is by using it in front of a word or phrase, you are highlighting that topic for other Twitter users to follow based on their common interest. It also offers a way for your tweets to get noticed. By using a hashtag your tweets come up as a search result when a user types in that particular keyword in the search box within Twitter. It's a great way to see real-time conversation around a particular topic, and it's also a great way to find new people discussing a topic of interest to you.

Anyone can make a hashtag for anything. For example, I use a hashtag for the Social Media for CEOs Boot Camps to stay connected with attendees after the event and to share key content pieces. It also provides a platform for the participants to share their thoughts, all while they connect with each other. The hashtag #SM4CEOs means nothing to anyone else on Twitter, but it creates a community of CEOs and business owners who are all learning about social media together—which makes it a great tool for networking. This type of community has no limitations because anyone reading this book who wants to learn more about social media and connect with other business owners can simply type in #SM4CEOs or even SM4CEOs without the hashtag in the search box and join in on the conversation.

Keep this in mind the next time you go to a live event or attend a webinar or podcast. Chances are a hashtag has been assigned to the event by the host. Try to watch for it as much as a week or a few days before the event and you'll be able to see who else is planning to attend and you can start to engage them online. Also, because they'll likely have a profile picture on their account, you'll be able to recognize them at the event, which makes starting a conversation or making an introduction very easy.

You may have noticed that TV shows are encouraging you to follow them on Twitter. They want you to watch the show in real time so you can be part of the conversation, which discourages you from fast-forwarding through the commercials if you watched the recorded version. A great example of this is the show Survivor. The host, Jeff Probst, is actually posting content about the show during the original broadcast and they have a special hashtag set up so that you can follow his comments as it relates to the show. This is a pretty creative way of securing viewership ratings and sponsorship dollars.

When it comes to using hashtags in your own tweets, do it sparingly. Don't fragment your conversation by overusing a hashtag and interrupting your content. A good example of what not to do would be this tweet; *How are all of my #NASCAR friends doing this #Friday morning? I have my #beer in my hand and I'm ready to watch my favorite #Ford car driver.* This is an example of an overuse of the hashtag. In addition, each time a word or phrase appears with a hashtag the color of the font is different from the rest of the content, which contributes to the interrupted feel of the tweet. Instead, use hashtags in proper context. For instance, if you want to share a well-known Franklin D. Roosevelt quote with your followers and observe Twitter etiquette, you would tweet, *"Be sincere, be brief, be seated." – Franklin D. Roosevelt #quotes.*

Setting Up Your Twitter Profile

The Twitter set-up video in the resource section of the Splash Media website can walk you through this in detail, but here are a few key elements to setting up a quality Twitter account.

- Choose an account name (handle) that best represents your brand (usually your company name). If that name is already assigned to someone else, try to find a variation of it. If you feel someone is inappropriately using or squatting on your desired account name, you can request Twitter have it released to you.

- Add a link to your website to make sure followers can easily learn more about you.

- Write a brief bio that is rich in keywords and key phrases (refer to your key phrase analysis). Describe the value you plan to deliver via your tweets. If you are creating a Twitter account for yourself as an individual, be sure to include something that reflects your personality. A study by HubSpot [March 11, 2009] indicated that Twitter accounts with bios attract eight times more followers than profiles without a bio.

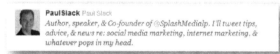

- Build a custom background that includes an avatar (digital representation of you). Most commonly, your avatar would be a photo of you or your company logo. Make sure you're mindful of the way you create your avatar. Here is an example of a restaurant that uses their logo along with their contact information and a list of their multiple locations.

The Tactical Wheel for Twitter

Listening

The first step in the Tactical Wheel is to listen, and there are several ways to do this on Twitter.

Use Key Phrases in Search Bar: By typing in key phrases from your key phrase analysis into the search bar, you will get results for real-time conversations and it will help you see the insights and opinions of other Twitter users who are discussing the key phrase. This is a great way to find people you might want to connect with. For example, I listen for people talking about "Social Media Companies/Firms/Agencies/Training/Help." This is also a great place for you to use those hashtags. In the search bar, attach the hashtag symbol to the beginning of the key phrases you want to listen for and see all of the users who have posted a tweet that included that hashtag. Remember to eliminate spaces when using the hashtag (#socialmedia not #social media).

Search Using the Advance Button: Advanced search on Twitter is hidden, but you need to know about it because it's a terrific tool for listening on Twitter. You can get to it by going here http://search.twitter.com/advanced. This feature will enable you to filter even further based on geography. For instance, you might run an Italian restaurant in a particular area and want to listen to everyone tweeting about food, pizza, dinner, etc. in your area. This opens up a great opportunity for targeting those people to follow and offer content such as recipes, promotions and special event notifications.

Create lists: You can sort and organize the people you follow and the content related to your business by creating specialized lists that will help you listen to just those users. For instance, you may have a list for the sports team in your area and anyone who tweets about them can become a marketing group for special promotions based on game days. This way you can listen by groups that have similar interests. Twitter users consider it a compliment to be included in Twitter lists because it signifies exclusivity and importance. As such, the number of lists you're on becomes a type of status symbol, so it is important to thank people who add you to one of their specialized lists.

Add people you follow to categorized lists by clicking "Add to List."

Building Community

You build community within Twitter when you find and engage with influencers and your target audience. It all starts with taking the first step of setting up a profile, using the search function with key phrases to find your audience, then following people who seem qualified. At first, you should expect about 20% of the people you follow to follow you back. Once you have a history of delivering value in your tweets and using some of the techniques described in this book, you'll see your percentages increase. Today, about 50% to 60% of the folks I follow will follow me back, but that's after lots of tweets and practice.

The basics to building community are you want to follow other people and offer useful information to encourage people to follow you. When you first start, be careful with regard to who you follow. Take a second to search through their profile and confirm that they tweet on a regular basis, that they re-tweet to others, and that they have a strong following relative to the number of tweets. Don't just follow people because they're following you.

Who *not* to follow on Twitter:

Too few tweets: If someone has 100 followers but they have only tweeted 2 times, you can assume they are new to Twitter and are just going out and trying to get followers before they have created a plan for adding value with quality content. They are not a good person to follow right now.

Too many tweets: The reverse is also true. Be leery of following someone who has 500 tweets on their profile but only 100 – 200 followers. Chances are their tweets are a lot of replies (@ reply) to random people in an attempt to earn followers, or they are pushing out automated self-promoting tweets (spam). You should take a pass on following them also.

Not enough followers: You will see people who are following 5000 people but they only have a couple of hundred people following them. They are probably using a spamming tool with the sole purpose of building a following, and not for adding value. You want to find people who have approximately the same number of people following them as they are following. The exception to this is with celebrities or well-known brands. They may have thousands (even hundreds of thousands) of followers but they are only following a hundred people. Consider this profile to be more like a Facebook Like (Fan) Page.

Finding Followers

When you think about whom you should follow, obvious people would be potential customers and influencers in your industry. Seek out these people by using the search tools on Twitter and through the use of hashtags. Once you follow them, find one of their recent tweets you feel would be relevant to your followers and re-tweet it. Next, go to their followers list and start following people who you think might be interesting to listen to or a potential client of yours. This will benefit you in two ways.

1. While the re-tweet is still one of your most recent entries on your profile, those new people you followed will see your profile as a new follower of theirs and they will also see that you re-tweeted someone they follow. This will make them more likely to follow you back without hesitation. In essence, who you know—and who knows you—is a powerful tool for gaining more followers. It is similar to a friend request on Facebook; you are more likely to accept a request from someone with whom you have friends in common than someone who appears to be a stranger.

2. The second reason for re-tweeting someone new (or any user, for that matter) is so when they broadcast a "thank you for re-tweeting me" tweet to you, all of their followers will see your name, which could lead to earning more followers simply from one re-tweet.

Who to Follow Tool: Twitter will suggest to you people you might want to follow based on the people you're already following. Twitter lists them in the Who to Follow section on the right-hand column of your Twitter account. Twitter uses algorithms that detect patterns in your account. For example, if you're following several moms, Twitter will suggest other profiles of moms for you to follow.

Twellow: Another great place to find followers is Twellow. com, which is a free tool that connects directly to Twitter and gives you the ability to use key phrases, titles, and industry sectors to identify people to follow.

Use Twellow.com to find individuals to follow by key phrase, title, location.

Google Search: You can also type specific search parameters into Google to find followers. For instance, if you wanted to find lawyers in Dallas who use Twitter, you can type in site:twitter.com/ *bio lawyer + Dallas, TX.

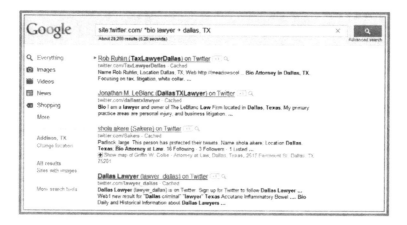

SplashCube: SplashCube enables you to set up monitoring campaigns using multiple key phrases to listen to conversations within Twitter. From SplashCube, you can follow individuals or reply directly to their tweets included the targeted key phrase.

Share Your Twitter URL: Be sure to make it very easy for people to follow you and your conversation by adding your Twitter URL to your email signatures, website pages, blog, business cards, coupons, YouTube videos, etc.

Broadcasting

Remember, the broadcasting section of the Tactical Wheel is all about posting content for your target market and engaging with others. Use Twitter to create a buzz around who you are and what value you bring to the table. You should be posting on Twitter (tweeting) at least once a day, which will give you visibility five to seven times a week. If you're posting less than once a day you might as well not post at all because you are invisible. The more visible and consistent you are, the more traffic you'll receive when you invite people to visit your blog or website.

Re-Tweets (RT): It's important to re-tweet people you admire in your industry. This creates an affinity with them and associates you with the audience you want to be connected to, which is referred to as social proofing. It also enables you to share useful information with your followers. To make it easy for others to re-tweet you, make sure you leave at least 15 unused characters so there is space for your Twitter account name to be included without having to abbreviate your original tweet. For example, because Twitter allows a maximum of 140 characters, try to limit your tweets to 125 characters. Although you can easily re-tweet by clicking on the re-tweet button next to someone's tweet, this function does not allow you to add your personality to the tweet. Instead, you may consider using the copy and paste functions on your computer to create a new tweet and add "(via @JohnSmith) Great content!" to the end of the tweet, which gives credit to the author and personalizes your tweet.

PaulSlack Paul Slack
Great insight - Ten ways to build your social media presence
http://bit.ly/rmvVUq via @JennyPescasio #SM4CEOs

@Replies: By starting a tweet with the @ symbol followed by a Twitter account name (with no blank spaces), you can direct a comment or question to one specific person that will appear publically for all of your followers to see. People like to be mentioned because it gives them the opportunity to be exposed to your followers and therefore earn new followers for themselves. It also improves your credibility because your followers see you engaging and adding value. Even if you are simply replying to a message from someone else, make sure your tweet makes sense to anyone who reads it. If your followers don't understand it they won't be interested in what you're sharing and won't join in on the conversation.

With @Replies there are very few barriers in the Twitter world versus the real world. You can easily start a conversation with a Fortune 500 CEO or have dinner with Charlie Sheen. Reply to and mention high-level influencers often and you'll never know what'll happen. Many times I've been able to have conversations with very high-level people just by mentioning them or even asking them a question.

Direct Messages (DM): Direct messaging is a less effective form of communication than @Reply, but it has its purpose. You want to use a direct message to communicate with someone privately. From a business perspective this typically happens when you're dealing with someone who's either saying something untrue about you through social media, or you have a customer who has expressed some concern and you want to deal with it offline. You always want to reply to them publically with a message such as "thank you for bringing this to our attention. We're excited about the opportunity to resolve it." The next correspondence should be via direct message to offer your phone number because you'd love to discuss it with them directly. Keep in mind that in order to use the Direct Message function, both accounts must be following each other, otherwise you cannot send a private message.

Ask questions: By asking powerful, open-ended questions you are more apt to get people to respond and engage with you. It allows the conversation to occur naturally. These questions should be relevant to your audience. Once you post a question you'll need to monitor Twitter closely so you can participate in the conversation your question sparks. Be sure to respond and thank those who answer. It is okay to post the same question throughout the day to make sure followers across the country can see it. Make sure your question is easy to answer within the 140 character limitation of a tweet. You don't want to ask a question that requires a lot of thought, either. Finally, remember to use hashtags to gain exposure, and offer to post everyone's answers in an upcoming blog. This typically gets the ball rolling. For example, *Mavs OR Heat. Good vs. Evil or just basketball? I'll post answers in an upcoming blog. #NBAFinals*

Promote Others: Let's take a page from Dale Carnegie's *How to Win Friends and Influence People* book. Don't just talk about your blog posts or your website. It's important to come off as informative and engaging, not commercial or self-centered. Again, remember: people like to talk about themselves. Give them a podium every once in a while to do that. Remember, too, that you're leading with value, so be as generous as possible with Twitter to point to other influencers in your industry that will be valuable to your target audience.

Help Others: Provide value by helping. People often express needs on Twitter and if you can ever connect a user with a resource that will help them solve a need, you've made a fan for life. Sometimes that solution will be your brand and sometimes it will be just brokering another relationship

"Follow Fridays" (#FF) & "Monday Mentions (#MM)": Use these hashtags on the appropriate days to promote influencers and followers. Add a word or two to describe why this person is worth following. It's also another way to give a shout out to recent followers. For instance, take the last handful of new followers who have at least 500 followers or more, and mention them on #FF or #MM with the intention of giving them more exposure and hoping they will do the same for you. This is a powerful way to gain visibility and deliver value at the same time. As a general rule, try to do this every Monday and Friday. For example, go to Twitter and search for either #FF or #MM on a Friday or Monday and you will find plenty.

Promote Your Blog, Website, and Products/Services: The

90/10 rule is 90% of what you broadcast should be useful and helpful to your followers and 10% can be promotional. This means one out of ten posts should include an offer or promotion. I'll get into this in more detail within the conversion section of this chapter. However, you should still promote your blog, website, and products/services within your tweets. Your blog is a resource. Your products/services help people and it's perfectly okay to talk about them in your tweets.

Edit Your Work: Although Twitter has a general spellcheck feature that shows a misspelled word, it will not pick up grammar issues, such as interchanging "there" with "their," so it's important to review and edit your tweets before you post them.

Abbreviations: As you might imagine, because we're dealing with 140 or fewer characters, there are a lot of abbreviations that are beginning to show up in Twitter. I don't recommend you craft your tweets with abbreviations in mind. Instead, you should write out the tweet as you would a regular sentence and then find ways of shortening it, if necessary.

Acceptable Abbreviations on Twitter

   & - and
   w/ - with
   thnx - thanks
   thru - through
   attn: - attention
   U - You (only if necessary)
   FF - Follow Fridays
   MM - Monday Mentions
   FB - Facebook

Developing Content

Twitter is all about the conversation. Simply pushing content out to others will not produce the level of engagement you need. Here are ways you can fully engage and add value through content.

Your Content: Tweet about a new blog post two to three times during the week you publish it, but not the same day. When you tweet about new product launches and special discounts on your website make sure you attach a link to the exact page that includes the call to action rather than just your home page. For tweets about your blog, use keywords and phrases from your blog headline, tweet about the topic and include the direct shortened URL. By using key words and phrases in the tweet, you have a better opportunity to be found. Experiment with putting hashtags in front of the key phrase. Be creative to optimize your traffic (click-through rate). Instead of tweeting "Read our blog – Top 5 Mistakes People Make When Buying Diamonds (*blog link*)," write "Top 5 Mistakes Made When Buying Diamonds. No. 3 will surprise you! (*blog link*)"

Curate Content: To avoid tweeting only about your own brand, find interesting stories, articles and blogs to share. This allows you to add value and keep readers engaged. Examples of items to curate include tweets, blog posts, online articles, and infographics. It's easy to curate other people's content by listening on Twitter, using your iGoogle account and reviewing the RSS feeds you have signed up for, as well as looking at the Google Alerts you set up as email notifications.

The only downside to promoting another blog or website in your tweets is you're linking to their environment and not yours.

This is okay, but to gain maximum benefit from curating content, it's best to first write a summary of the blog post or article you want to curate inside your own blog. Be sure to include a link within the summary to the content you are referencing. Mention the summary in your tweet and then drive people to your blog where they can read the summary, and provide a link in the blog back to the original article.

Tweet Photos: Just as with Facebook, photos get people's attention more easily than other content. Sign up for twitpic.com and tweet fun, informative, or interesting photos to your followers. Not only is it a great way to add something new but people will more easily join a conversation with you and re-tweet you.

Strategies for Effective and Efficient Tweets

When you first start out on Twitter you may find an hour has passed and you're not exactly sure if it was well spent or if you can commit that much time just to Twitter. That's when a solid strategy will make all the difference.

Prime Tweeting Hours: Dan Zarella is considered a viral marketing scientist who has conducted elaborate research online to determine the best way to tweet and get re-tweeted. Based on his research, the strongest hours for re-tweets are in the late afternoons on Thursday and Friday (Eastern Time). That doesn't mean you shouldn't be tweeting throughout the day and week, but if you have a new product to launch or a great blog post to share make sure you tweet about it during the prime hours. Most often people check Twitter in the morning (8:00 a.m. – 9:00 a.m.), in the late afternoon (1:00 p.m. - 4:00 p.m.)

and the evenings (after 8:00 pm) in their time zone, so take full advantage of these times.

Schedule Your Tweets: Whether you are tweeting about a new blog post, sharing a good quote, or curating content from other sites, you can easily schedule your tweets in advance by using tools such as HootSuite, SplashCube, and TweetDeck. These sites help you take advantage of prime tweeting times without interrupting your productivity. The other advantage to pre-scheduling your tweets is to avoid being a "noisy tweeter," which is when your tweets appear on your follower's Twitter stream every one to two minutes. No one wants their entire screen filled up with just your avatar and your tweets. Space out your tweets to give people time to react and engage. Take the prime re-tweeting times into account and schedule your blog post tweets in the late afternoon, an interesting quote in the morning and curated content in the mid-afternoon. This will add variety to the tweet stream on your profile while allowing you to thank people and @reply during various times in between.

Optimize the Order of Your Tweets: Although Twitter can appear to be a random flow of information you should make sure you are optimizing your visibility to potential new followers. For instance, when someone sees your name mentioned by someone they are following or notices that you are following them, they make a quick decision about whether they want to follow you back based on the same criteria you're using. They'll click on your account profile and quickly scan your latest tweets. Therefore, the last tweet of the morning or evening should lead with value and not be a generic entry.

When you go on Twitter for a 15-minute or 30-minute session, make the most of it. For instance, you may set out with the intention to post a tweet about your blog with a link, check in to see who mentioned you, who asked you a question, or who re-tweeted you. If you post your blog tweet first, then reply to someone and finish by thanking everyone who re-tweeted you, your tweet stream on your profile will show the least significant tweets first and your blog post will have been pushed down the page so far a new follower has to scroll down to see it. In this scenario, the likelihood that your blog would get noticed is very small. However, if you took care of the re-tweet thank yous and replies first, then found new people to follow and finished your session by posting your blog link, the most important value-add would occupy primary real estate on your profile. That way any potential new followers will see your blog first and foremost and they would also see you engaging in conversation with others. Now you are a prime candidate for them to follow and re-tweet.

Shortened URL Service: Because of the character limit on Twitter, you'll need to shorten the long URL to your blog. You also want to be able to measure the amount of traffic you're getting from your efforts (click-through rate), which is where a shortened URL service comes in handy. Bit.ly is one of the most popular sites to use and, based on Dan Zarella's research it is also one of the most frequently re-tweeted link services compared to ow.ly, tinyurl.com, etc.

Bit.ly also helps you monitor and manage your traffic in other ways. First, it provides you with hourly and daily tracking of the number of clicks you receive on your link, from what platform the traffic is originating (Twitter, Facebook) and which locations are re-tweeting you (U.S., UK, Jamaica, etc.). It also shows you every person who used your bit.ly and tweeted or re-tweeted your content. This is a great way to easily see who to thank and follow, as well as get ideas of how other people are tweeting the content. Finally, you can see what hashtags people used when they tweeted your content to their followers. This gives you an idea for new hashtag groups to follow and use in your own tweets. You can also check out who is engaging using that hashtag, which will provide you with new, relevant people to follow.

SplashCube – SplashCube was first developed by Splash Media to help our social media managers become as efficient as possible. As you've probably gathered from this book, there's a lot of art and science that goes into successful social media marketing. We wanted to take as much of the guesswork out of managing our clients' environments as possible. We also wanted to deliver best-in-class services. There wasn't a tool in the market that did what we wanted, so we decided to build our own. What makes SplashCube unique is it actually compares your social media environment to best-in-class environments in real time. Based upon that analysis, it taps into a database of best practices and prescribes tasks you can take within Twitter, Facebook, and LinkedIn to align your environment with those we consider best in class. This keeps you from ever having to guess what you should be doing within Twitter or the other platforms at any moment in time. It also provides contextual videos to train users how best to implement recommended tasks.

Conversion

Your primary goals on Twitter are to be seen as an industry expert and to encourage people to go to your website and take action based on an offer that might exist on your blog or a featured product page. The bait are your tweets and the hooks are your offers. This only works if you lead with value first and remember the 90/10 rule. Twitter is a great place to generate opportunities for your business mainly because people are talking about their wants and needs. However, if you are perceived as a hungry salesman and not a social media concierge, then your tweets will seem like interruptions and not help.

You also need to keep in mind the shelf life of tweets lasts about as long as the spoken word. It's there and then it's gone for the most part. To be effective in converting people on Twitter you need to be thoughtful about offers that would appeal to your target audience. For instance, if your business is a restaurant you'll want to listen for people in your city talking about where to go for dinner so you can @reply to them with a link to a coupon that exists on your blog that they can bring into the restaurant and get a special offer.

B2B companies, or any company, wanting to generate leads for their business will have success in Twitter by tweeting offers for things like e-books, free analysis/consultations, access to research, and promoting events like webinars, seminars, or lunch-and-learns.

Our Splash Media retail and ecommerce clients have experienced a lot of success running Twitter-only promotions that feature a coupon to buy a product and get a special pricing or shipping discount.

Special Twitter offer to receive a free pendant. When user clicks on offer they land on a page with a printable coupon.

Twitter can become one of the most effective social media platforms for your business. Twitter is the most convenient place to listen and find people to connect with on your journey to turning friends into customers and customers into evangelists. If you'll follow the steps in this chapter, you can build an amazingly vibrant community and generate leads by jumping in to help prospective customers solve their problems.

Social Rules - Twitter:

Rule # 42: Twitter is the lowest barrier to entry social media platform and the best for listening.

Rule #43: Listen on Twitter by using the Advance Search button and create lists of specific groups of people whose conversations you want to monitor.

Rule #44: Build your community by following people. Use the follow-the-followers technique to grow your followers quickly.

Rule #45: Do not follow people whose profile indicates they engage in spam or whose tweets are primarily self-promoting posts.

Rule #46: Broadcasting within Twitter requires you to consistently engage with others. Use the techniques of re-tweeting, @reply, #FollowFridays, #MondayMentions, asking questions and promoting others to gain visibility and credibility for your brand.

Rule #47: Use these top three strategies for developing content on Twitter: Post headlines of your blogs and videos multiple times, curate other people's content, use hashtags with key phrases, and share photos.

Rule #48: Use scheduling software like SplashCube, TweetDeck, or HootSuite to easily plan your tweets throughout the prime tweeting hours without interrupting your productivity.

Rule #49: Promote active calls to action and run Twitter-only promotions to convert followers to prospects and customers.

14. LINKEDIN

Did you ever have a Rolodex on your desk? You remember that amazing feat of technology that enabled you to find critical information about business contacts within a relatively short amount of time. By critical information I am referring to the most essential details such as their name, their company and their phone number. If you're like me, you probably taped or stapled business cards to a blank rolodex card to save you from having to rewrite the information. You probably wrote other key facts on the back, like the name of their spouse, their kids, their birthday or where they went to college.

Invented in 1956, the Rolodex was a major improvement to business contact retrieval. Prior to its existence, most business people had to sort through stacks of business cards that were rubber-banded together, or a file cabinet with client folders, or worse yet, the phonebook to dig up basic contact information. I'm sure an even greater advancement in business contact information had to be the business card itself. The business card served a dual purpose; it enabled business people to promote themselves and their companies while it allowed the recipient to store pertinent information about a business in a convenient way.

I remember as a young and green salesman, meeting a key prospect from one of the large phone companies for the very first time. In our meeting, as he was grabbing a business card from his desk drawer, he shared with me that he had been with the company for more than twenty years and he was still using the business cards originally issued to him. I found that pretty interesting and had visions of him sitting at that very same desk for the past twenty years. Then he began scratching through each line on the card with a pen because his contact information had changed. In fact, I think the only thing left unmarked when he was done was his name. He wrote all of his new information on the back of the card and gave it to me, smiling. I took his scribbled up card back to my office and added it to my Rolodex, thinking how silly he had been for not having new business cards printed as his contact information changed. Over time as I played the scene back in my head, I realized he was trying to communicate to me how frugal he was and I wouldn't do much business with him unless I could help him be frugal with the company.

The Rolodex Revamped

Staying on top of important contact information while enabling potential customers and vendors to connect you has never been easier, thanks to LinkedIn. LinkedIn achieves the two basic purposes of the business card, plus adds the convenience of the old fashioned Rolodex and much more.

I started my LinkedIn profile in 2004 and since then I've grown it to more than 2000 connections. I have more than 25 recommendations on my LinkedIn profile, and over 300 people—many of them potential customers—visit my profile each and every month. Most of the people who visit find my LinkedIn profile do so as a result of searches using key phrases I've used to optimize my profile. I participate in over 15 groups and I also manage a group for Splash Media. My profile is probably worth $1 million or more to me when you consider the connections, new visitors, and credibility it delivers for Splash Media and my personal brand. If you'll follow the steps outlined in this chapter, you can establish a presence on LinkedIn that can be every bit as valuable for your business.

> Why Business Owners Use LinkedIn
>
> Beyond just passing along contact information and enabling a business to promote itself like a business card, LinkedIn provides business owners many great opportunities.
>
> Finding prospects.
>
> Giving answers to questions and inquiries, which allows you to consistently add value,
>
> Building third-party credibility, which acts as word-of-mouth advertising on steroids and is the essence of what makes social media so special today,
>
> Generating leads for your business,
>
> Getting answers to questions you may not be able to find in other avenues or other sources.
>
> Researching potential customers, as well as gaining pre-meeting background information on an individual.
>
> Finding employees.

LinkedIn as a Gold Mine for Leads

One of the key benefits to LinkedIn is its ability to help your company find and acquire new customers. What makes it so effective is everyone on LinkedIn is responsible for keeping their own information up to date and they have a vested interest in doing so because they're looking for new business—just like you. This makes it infinitely better than buying a lead list to help you prospect. If you've ever purchased a lead list then you've probably discovered 10% to 20% of the information is inaccurate. What I've found when I purchased them was, in many cases, the organization was still in business but the key contacts had moved on or the organizational structure itself had changed. This makes LinkedIn one of the best possible places to fish for new business, especially if you sell to businesses. However, if you are a B2C company or a retailer, don't count LinkedIn out. Your best customers have jobs and you can find them on LinkedIn.

Connecting Using LinkedIn Search Feature

At the heart of LinkedIn is also a very powerful search engine that makes it easy for you to look for individuals by keyword, by their title within the organization or their industry. You can do searches for their seniority level, size of their company, their city, the college they went to and even the groups they're involved in.

If you're familiar with LinkedIn, you'll notice there's a search bar at the very top of the screen that gives you many options for searching through different filters. Within the search bar there's a drop-down menu with "People" as the default setting. When you click on the arrow of the menu you'll discover there are more options than just people. Before typing in your key phrase for your search, click on the Advanced button for even more choices, such as titles, companies, etc. The search feature will help you connect with potential buyers and clients based on your desired filters rather than general criteria.

As with any type of networking, an effective strategy for making connections is to find common ground with people such as college alumni, former employers, or various community or social groups. A great advantage to connecting with people is when you send someone an invitation to connect it doesn't just show up in their account; it also sends an email message. This gives you the ability to send an email to someone you want to connect with without knowing their email address.

Setting up Your Personal Profile

Your profile on LinkedIn is more than a duplication of your résumé; it is more like a personal brochure. Although you should include the information that generally appears in a résumé you should think of your profile in terms of where you'd like to go rather than where you've already been. Keep it current and change your position as your status changes; be sure to update the different organizations and groups you become involved with as well. When you make these changes they will appear in the LinkedIn update email messages that are sent to people who are connected with you. It makes you more visible to your LinkedIn network keeping you top of mind.

Key resources for creating your profile

- Use your most recent résumé or a summary biography document as a sound reference point.*
- Use a good, current profile picture.
- Have an inventory of the groups and associations you participate in.
- Use your key phrase analysis document for descriptive ways to talk about your career.
- A good friend and trusted colleague of mine, Mike O'Neil, offers a terrific LinkedIn profile worksheet at www.rocktheworldbook.com/extras.

*LinkedIn doesn't have a spellcheck and has very small windows for typing in information. Therefore, working from a worksheet that has spellcheck saves you time and errors; just copy and paste your information into your profile.

The most important part of your profile is the headline. The challenge is you have 120 characters to tell your story about what you do for your company and it is important to be able to describe yourself while still including key phrases. You need to include your title, key words that are relevant to you and a value statement.

Sample Effective LinkedIn Headlines

- CEO, Nonprofit Fundraising Expert, 501c3 Expert. I will raise $10,000 to $50,000 for your nonprofit—guaranteed.
- President and CEO, Newell Anderson Enterprises
- CEO, COO, President, Corporate Development Global Fortune 500 Leader, a Dynamic Leader with 80 Acquisitions.
- Social Media Marketing Guru & Chief Learning Officer at Splash Media; Social Media Marketing/Education Firm

As you're developing the rest of your profile consider using action words, key phrases, and descriptive text, listing all of your current occupations and significant volunteer activities, and integrating your blog and Twitter accounts.

Setting Up Your Company Profile

Setting up your company profile is equally as important as your personal profile. The purpose of your company profile is to promote your business and just like your personal profile, your company should be forward thinking, talking about the product or services you provide and creating another way for people to connect with you. LinkedIn offers a great set-up wizard that makes it easy to create your basic information such as description, number of employees and your industry. It's also very simple to add your logo, different branch locations, pull your blog from your website and show your Twitter profile stream in real time.

Once your company profile is complete LinkedIn will pull in a variety of other information, such as job postings, a list of current and former employees, any new hires that have recently joined your organization, recent promotions, the median age of your staff, number of employees, top schools represented and much more.

Also set up your company products and services, which is an option on the company profile tab. Complete the form entering all of the relevant data, such as product information, images, and videos that tells the story of how you can provide value to your customers.

Once on your company page, select Products and Services then click on Add a product & service button.

LinkedIn gives members the ability to search for companies using keywords, so be sure to use your key phrase analysis to create descriptive text for your business and your products and services.

Optimizing Groups

There are more than 375,000 groups in LinkedIn and there are two important ways to leverage these groups to gain exposure, build community, and ultimately drive traffic back to your website or blog.

Become part of relevant groups in your industry so you have a voice and a place where you can express your thoughts and opinions as it relates to your industry. These industry groups will give you common ground with the other members, making it much easier to connect. The LinkedIn groups you're a member of also become a place for you to broadcast content to a highly targeted audience. If done correctly, this can become one of your best sources of traffic. When looking for groups to join, find groups where you can be the representative for your industry. This is better than being in groups full of your competitors. For example, I'm a member of about 15 groups and while some are industry related, many are groups where my best prospects go to stay up to date within their domain of responsibility, such as groups exclusively for C-levels, VP's of Marketing/Sales, or Entrepreneurs. This way you become the go-to-guy in that group for all things related to your industry. You should seek out and find 15 or more groups to join. Beyond building awareness and delivering thought leadership, you'll also gain potential connections through other members.

Start a group tailored to your target audience. Starting a group of your own is the best place within LinkedIn to build community and engage with customers and potential customers. Unlike Facebook, your company profile on LinkedIn is very limited in terms of other people commenting and your ability to respond. Setting up your own group is an excellent workaround. However, remember to lead with value and create a group to benefit your target audience by providing a platform for them to share questions and you to share knowledge. The name of the group should not be the name of your company, but instead be focused around the value members will receive by joining. For example, [*Industry Topic*] Tips, Tricks, & Advice. With a name like this, you'll show up when people are looking for groups to join around the topic and you are also communicating the value they'll receive by joining your group. At Splash Media, we have a group called Social Media Boot Camp for CEOs. This is tied to the educational events we host across the country and gives past attendees a way to stay connected with us and to get their questions answered. For us it's a way to extend the reach of our event and continue to maintain relationships with previous attendees who might someday become clients. Feel free to join our group, even if you haven't attended one of our boot camps.

Once you create a group, start a discussion at least once a week with relevant topics and then ask for input or feedback from the group. Once the group gets to about 200 or more members it will begin to take on a life of its own with members starting the discussions and helping each other out, which is perfectly fine. The 90/10 rule is critical here. If your members view you as a billboard they will tune you out and the group will lose its effectiveness.

The Tactical Wheel for LinkedIn

Listening

There are three places within LinkedIn where you'll find good fruit in terms of listening.

1. **LinkedIn Answers.** This is an area within LinkedIn where users can pose questions and solicit answers, which makes it an important place to listen in for conversations that are important to you. To listen, go to the search bar, click on Answers and search for questions related to your industry. It will show you answers that have already been posted as well as questions still soliciting responses. You can do

key phrase searches to find pertinent questions to answer as a way to demonstrate your expertise, gain exposure, and establish your credibility. Trending key phrases can produce good questions about current topics. In the next example, I searched for "B2B Google Plus" and found three current relevant questions.

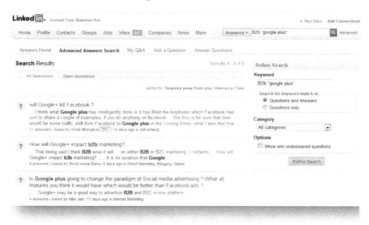

A search for a trending key phrase in my industry produced 3 good questions to answer and deliver thought leadership.

Within the LinkedIn Answers home page, you can select categories of questions for specific industries and add those categories to your RSS reader, such as iGoogle Reader. This way you can easily monitor questions by category each time you log into your RSS Reader, so you can contribute comments and respond with answers quickly and easily.

2. **LinkedIn Signals.** This feature under the News section enables you to easily monitor the LinkedIn status updates by you, your connections, or the connections of your connections. From the Signals section you can also like, comment, or share these status updates. You can type in key phrases in the search bar and monitor status updates by topic.

3. **New Group Discussions**. The third place to benefit from listening is by reading new discussions from relevant groups. Look at the different discussions started within groups you belong to, including your own, and listen for conversations happening within groups outside those you belong to offers great opportunities to build community and share your knowledge. Remember the primary purpose of listening in social media is to identify influencers, partners, customers, and potential customers to connect with, as well as finding conversations you can jump into and deliver value.

Listening for conversations within the groups you belong to is simple. In most cases you'll receive emails from LinkedIn with summaries of discussions. You can also visit the group page and see active discussions. However, you'll have to go over to Google to find discussions in other groups. In the Google search bar, type in site:linkedin.com/groups [key phrase]. This will bring back only discussions within LinkedIn groups that include the key phrase. If you select a time range in the left column of the search result, you'll see current discussions. In the following example, by typing in a key phrase and then selecting Past 24 hours in the left column, I found 64 active discussions within LinkedIn groups related to the key phrase. I can now look at these discussions and try to connect with the individuals participating or participate myself.

A search in Google produced 64 discussions within LinkedIn groups over the last 24 hours.

Building Community

Here are the key ways to build community through LinkedIn:

1. **Invite group members to connect with your personal profile.** LinkedIn allows you to request connections from users who are members of the same group. You can easily find these potential connections by using the Advanced Search feature and selecting Group Members under the Relationship category. Because there are over 100 million users from all over the world using LinkedIn, you can also narrow down potential connections by using a title and selecting a location.

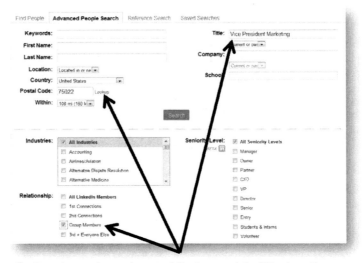

On the advanced search page, I like to search by Title, Location, and Group Members.

The result from the above search generated over 1600 potential connections. Now I can simply request a connection from the individuals who appear in the results and use our shared group membership as common ground. This is done by clicking the *Add to network* link on the right side of the individual's result.

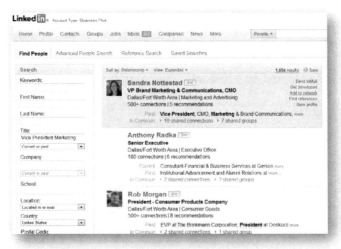

The advanced search result identifies the number of shared connections and groups. You can also save a search and come back another time for more community building.

2. **Upload your customer and prospect database,** and invite people to connect that way. You can also upload that same database and invite those people to join your LinkedIn group(s).

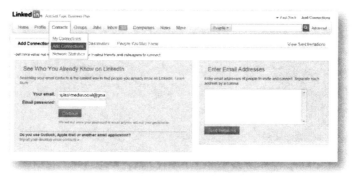

LinkedIn can use your address book or you can upload your customer and prospect database to find connections.

3. **Turn LinkedIn into your personal Rolodex** – Whenever you meet someone in a business setting look them up on LinkedIn and send them a connection request. Also, it's time to throw away that stack of business cards you have stashed away in file cabinets and desk drawers. Go through each card and look up the individuals to see if they are on LinkedIn. My guess is most of them are by now. Send them a connection request and then toss the business card in the trash. Once they're connected to you, you will be more top of mind and they'll be able to follow your activity on LinkedIn.

A few years ago, after reading a book on getting more organized, I decided to go through some old files and purge items I hadn't touched in years. I still had old customer and prospect files from previous positions that were over 10 years old! As I cleaned out the files, I looked up old contacts in LinkedIn and was able to find nearly all of them. One person in particular had been the president of a company I used to call on. He sold his company and was now semi-retired and doing some consulting work on the side. I would have never been able to find him if it weren't for LinkedIn. But, because we are all responsible for keeping our profiles up to date, LinkedIn made it easy for me to find and connect with him.

Shortly after we connected, he reached out and asked to grab some coffee to get caught up. It had been about six years since we had spoken in person. When I shared with him what I was up to, he told me about a client of his in Utah who really needed my help. Shortly after our meeting he set up a conference call for an introduction. The next thing I know, his client is on a plane to Dallas to meet me and see my operation. For the next two years, this referral became my biggest customer by far.

Landing this big client would have never happened without LinkedIn, and it all started with a simple connection request from a dusty business card in a file cabinet. It's about time you start turning your old business card collection into revenue for your business, too.

Broadcasting

A primary purpose of LinkedIn is to lasso users over to your environment by broadcasting useful information along with timely calls to action and links to your blog. There are two main ways to broadcast within LinkedIn:

1. **Update your status every business day of the week.** Get in the habit of posting a status update first thing in the morning. As mentioned earlier, the people connected to you will see your status update change on their home page. Think of yourself as the expert within your industry to your

connections and it's your job to keep them up to date. At least two times per week include relevant information you curated from the web that would interest your customers. This could be an article from an industry website or major publication, an interesting video from YouTube, or an infographic. Be sure to promote new blog articles as a status update, but unlike Twitter, only post it one time. You can save the rest of your updates to ask open-ended questions, share what you're working on, or make a special offer.

2. **Broadcast your blog and video content to your groups.** If you set your personal profile and company profile up correctly, each time you publish a new blog article it will show up within these areas. However, you have a tremendous opportunity to promote your blog articles inside LinkedIn by broadcasting them within the groups you participate in. The LinkedIn Word Press plug-in makes this possible. When you're ready to broadcast a blog article, first log into your LinkedIn account, then go to the article on your blog and click the Share button. A wizard will appear prompting you to start a discussion about the article and then gives you the ability to select LinkedIn groups you are a member of to broadcast the article. If you have joined at least 15 groups and you are actively providing value, you'll find this tactic one of your favorite traffic-building techniques for your blog.

Step 1: Use the LinkedIn Word Press plug in to one touch publish blogs to all of your groups.

Step 2: The article now appears inside the selected group(s).

Developing Content

There are four places to create content within LinkedIn that will help you increase exposure, share value, and generate conversions.

1. **Starting and responding to group discussions.** As mentioned earlier, start a discussion in your group at least once each week. By definition, discussions are conversations about a topic. A healthy discussion should have multiple responses. Discussions asking for opinions, help, or input tend to work well. You can also attach links to content outside the group, so consider curating an article and asking people if they agree with the author's opinion. You can also post links to your blog or video and

ask for feedback and opinions. In the following example, I started a discussion by asking the group if they had any burning questions about social media and received 28 comments, each with topics to discuss. This information was passed on to the blogging team at Splash Media and turned into a content plan. Each week we answered one of those topics as a blog article.

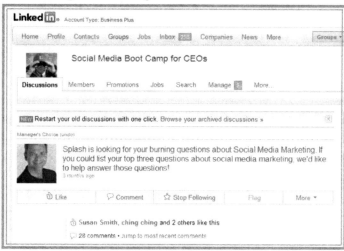

2. **Posting Events.** This is a great way to generate content but is often overlooked by businesses. Remember, people use the Internet to formulate buying criteria and to make informed buying decisions. People want to be educated, and hosting events to share your knowledge and help potential customers make informed decisions will enable you to connect with them. Consider hosting a monthly webinar that walks potential customers through the top ten questions everybody should ask themselves before purchasing [whatever your product or service is]. When you promote this event in LinkedIn, you'll be able to see users who plan to attend as well as users interested in

attending. These folks are leads! Regardless of whether or not they attend the event.

3. **Listing job openings.** LinkedIn is probably most known as a recruiting tool and my hope is that after reading this chapter, you'll be convinced it's much more than that. It is true, however, that finding quality candidates on LinkedIn can be valuable for your business. At Splash Media, we've recruited about 75% of our team from LinkedIn.

4. **Using LinkedIn Answers for content.** When you find a question to answer go write a blog post that provides a detailed response to the question. In the Answers section, provide a concise answer, but at the end of your answer say something like "I've written a blog on this topic that provides a lot more information with links to useful resources." Then include a link to the blog article. This way you're driving them over to your environment.

Conversion

Just as with all of the different social media platforms, you tee up conversions by first leading with value and building trust. Once you've been established as a value provider, you're in an excellent position to promote special offers within LinkedIn. Here are some examples to try:

Send an announcement to your group. LinkedIn allows you to send an announcement to everyone in your group once a week. Announcements show up in your members' email even if you don't have their email address. This can be much more effective than email marketing because you're a trusted source for information. If you use this strategy sparingly, no more than once per month and make a really compelling offer, you'll generate conversions. Avoid hype and tie the offer to the fact that they are part of the group. Here are some examples:

"Because you have been a member of the [name of group] I wanted to make you aware that we just got in an extra shipment of [product] that wasn't supposed to get here until [sometime in the future]. We don't have room in our warehouse to store the shipment, so if you've been in the market for [product], click the attached link to learn more."

"Last time I was in Italy, I purchased 20 cases of 2003Brunello di Montalcino Chianti. It is considered by many to be the best Chianti in the world. Because you are a trusted friend and member of our [name of group] I wanted to personally offer a bottle to you at 50% off the wine list price next time you stop by for dinner. When you make your reservation, simply mention the name of this group and I will have a bottle waiting for you at your table. Please let me know how you liked the wine by commenting in our group discussion."

"In August we will be launching a brand new software product that [describe what it does], but prior to that we would like to make it available exclusively to the members of our group for free for the next 90 days. All we ask in return is for you to let us know what you think and any new features you would like us to add to the product."

Make offers in your status update. Periodically within your status update, make an offer for something of value. Think in terms of creating an electronically or digitally delivered item (e-book, white paper, smartphone app, etc.) that could help users make an informed buying decision or formulate their buying criteria.

Use the SlideShare plug-in to generate a free ad. Through the

SlideShare application you can upload a PowerPoint document to your profile page. What I like to do is create a one slide PowerPoint with a visual call to action and upload that to my profile page via SlideShare. This becomes a free ad on my LinkedIn profile page. You can take any advertising creative idea and do this yourself. For example, a restaurant could post its menu or an advertised special. A software company could post "Buy three licenses and get two free."

Regardless of the industry you're in, whether you are selling cars or super computers or own a small elegant restaurant, LinkedIn is an important site for you to find and connect with your customers and potential customers. Use the tactics outlined in this chapter and see what tapping into over 100 million users can do for your business.

Social Rules - LinkedIn:

Rules #50: Joining 10-15 relevant groups and using these groups to promote your blog articles and videos will grow your traffic significantly.

Rule #51: Optimize your personal and company profiles with key phrases.

Rule #52: Set up your own group designed to educate and help your target audience. Use this group to promote your blog and video content.

Rule #53: Listen and participate in conversations by using LinkedIn Answers to help solve your target market's questions.

Rule #54: Use Advanced Search to identify group members and

invite them to connect with your personal profile. Invite your database to join you on LinkedIn.

Rule #55: Broadcasting on LinkedIn consists of updating your status every day.

Rule #56: Once each month promote an active call to action as a status update.

15. YOUTUBE

Back in 2006, when Google purchased one-and-a-half-year-old YouTube for $1.65 billion dollars, I wasn't surprised because Google had been making a lot of acquisitions the previous year. What was surprising is that collectively, Google had spent $150 million to acquire 15 companies, not one single platform. The price tag was shocking. A giant acquisition such as YouTube made people take notice, especially given YouTube's short time online.

One thing that I've always known about Google, ever since they came out with AdWords, is at the end of the day, Google isn't a search engine as much as they are an advertising network that happens to use search as their primary way to attract an audience. Because they are an advertising network it made sense that they'd want to acquire YouTube because it was the number one visited video site on the web at the time, even as young as they were. But as I mentioned, I was surprised by the price. They paid nearly $2 billion dollars for this company, which seemed too high even though YouTube had a lot of traffic and Google could put their ads on the website and make money. But for $2 billion it would take a long time to recoup their investment.

Then one day it all came together. It's amazing the things you can learn from your kids. Shortly after hearing the news of the acquisition I walked past the upstairs den in my house and out of the corner of my eye I saw all three of my little kids huddled around the family computer. I remember thinking that's not something you see every day—all three of your kids together, interested in the same thing, at the same time. If you're a parent, you understand that strange sixth-sense warning you get sometimes that starts with the hairs rising on the back of your neck. That's exactly what happened as I was taking in the scene. I decided to take a closer look and what I saw amazed me. They were watching reruns of cartoons on YouTube. That's when it hit me like a ton of bricks. YouTube was much more than just a video sharing, video uploading network... YouTube was becoming the next television!

Fast-forward to 2011, when the line between television and the Internet is greatly blurred with things like GoogleTV and Apple's Internet Television. In fact, many TVs and most gaming systems come with Internet Television built in. Looking back at my children watching TV from the computer was one of those a-ha moments for me. I saw the future of the web and how we would begin to access any content we wanted wherever and whenever we wanted. We were truly becoming a content-on-demand society.

Why Your Business Needs Video

So why would your business need video as part of your social media content strategy?

Tell your story in a growing platform. Neilson Ratings estimate that by 2014, 90% of all of our web traffic will be video. This may seem aggressive but consider this: video remains the most compelling way to tell a company's story. It's a great platform for communicating with potential customers. In addition, with the rise of the smartphone and other mobile devices like The Tablet and the iPad, your customers can connect with you anywhere. Video can take your company's story to wherever your potential customers are and give you an edge over your competition.

People would rather watch the Internet than read it. If you think about it, the Internet has succeeded over the past 15 years despite the fact we've had to read everything. Now that we can watch it like a television we would rather watch it than read it. The largest companies in the world have already jumped on this growing trend. According to a recent study by Burson-Marsteller, the amount of YouTube videos Fortune 100 companies are producing on a monthly basis actually exceeds the number of blogs they are posting. The average Fortune 100 Company is creating and posting ten YouTube videos per month versus only seven blog posts per month.

The largest companies in the world are spending a lot of time, energy and resources to understand the best possible places for finding, acquiring and engaging their customers. Because they've discovered their customers would rather watch the Internet than read it, they're producing a lot of YouTube video and so should you.

The good news for you is I doubt your competition has figured this one out yet. If you can commit to doing at least one video a month, by the time your competition figures out how much video content consumers watch online, you'll be so far ahead of them they won't catch up with you anytime soon. I have GoogleTV at home and watch as much video from the Internet as I do from my cable provider. Many of you would never be able to afford a commercial that would show up on my television the old fashioned way, but now you have access to it via web video. I have watched a lot of corporate videos on my TV from YouTube and other video sites. This is a huge opportunity for your business.

Maximize Search Engine Optimization. Another advantage of why video should be part of your social media content strategy is the search engine optimization impact. You've probably noticed when you do searches on Google today videos are among the top-ranked results. There's a reason for that. *BusinessWeek* published an article in 2010 about how video is 53 times more likely to appear on the first page of Google than any other type of content. According to *BusinessWeek,* your video will give you another opportunity to rank well on the largest search engine in the world. Therefore, having video as part of your social media marketing strategy, you'll be attracting customers from YouTube, TVs and mobile devices across the globe, as well as Google. No other media has that kind of reach.

YouTube Stats for Business

- Second-largest search engine in the world.
- Over 2 billion videos are viewed each day
- Over 70% of people watching these videos are age 18 or older.

If you want an opportunity to show up in the No. 1 and No. 2 search engines in the world, you have to use video. It's the only way you'll get a good ranking in YouTube and it will help you out quite a bit over Google. Because YouTube is the second largest search engine, there are more searches conducted at YouTube than Yahoo or Bing, and there is less competition which is a huge opportunity.

Consider these search results as evidence of the power of YouTube to get your business noticed.

- Search for "what is CRM software?" At YouTube, only 5000 videos show up. If you go to Google and do that very same search, you get over three million pieces of web content that you'd have to compete with. If you are a CRM software company, wouldn't you want to have a video that was titled and tagged "what is CRM software" so you'd have a great opportunity to rank extremely high for your targeted audience?

- Search for "how to make salsa." Only 5400 videos pop up for that key phrase in YouTube, but 30 million pieces of content show up over at Google. I don't know about you, but I think I'd prefer to learn how to make salsa by watching someone rather than reading a recipe.

- Search for "best surround sound systems." 2100 videos pop up on YouTube versus six million pieces of content on Google.

If you haven't started making videos to tell your company's story, you need to seriously consider creating videos that people want to watch because the importance of video will only grow over time.

Two Video Success Stories

If you haven't already read it, you should pick up a copy of the book, *Crush It!* written by Gary Vanerychuck. In his book, Gary shares the details about how he took his dad's liquor store business in New York from about $4 million in annual revenue to more than $50 million in eight years by leveraging social media. He understood that people would rather watch the Internet than read it, so video was an important part of his strategy. He discovered people walking into the liquor store in this blue collar part of New York City had no clue what kind of wine to buy to pair with food or to bring to a dinner party. Gary had been working in the store since he was young and he realized customers were making blind buying decisions. Gary decided he would create videos for the average Joe to help people understand wine pairings without sounding like a wine snob. He committed to doing one video a day, every single day of the week, where he compared three different bottles of wine. In very layman terms he described how they tasted and what types of food they would complement. With the introduction of those videos and the personality he brought to the customer experience, the videos went viral and his father's liquor store business exploded. If you want to see how easily he's producing the videos, check out WineLibrary.tv.

Blendtec is another case study that demonstrates the amazing power video can have for your business. Blendtec is a relatively small manufacturer of high-end blenders, mostly for commercial use at restaurants. One thing Blendtec understood early on was people would rather watch the blenders in action than read about their features.

The Blendtec CEO, Tom Dickson, decided to create a channel that showcased the incredible power of their blenders by taking non-food items and blending them into dust. They've blended everything from magnets to iPhones, golf clubs, and even an iPad, and literally turned these items to dust in these videos. It's had a tremendous impact on their sales. According to Blendtec, in the first five days of launching their channel, they had over seven million views and their sales increased by over 700%!

How to Create a Remarkable Video

There are two paths you use to create videos to grow your

business, and each has its pros and cons. The first way is to create your own homemade, user-generated video. The other way is to have a professional company actually create the videos for you.

Homemade Videos

To create your own videos you can simply use a digital video camera available at most big-box retailers. Once you shoot the footage you have to edit it yourself, which you can do with various video-editing software on the market, such as Microsoft Movie Maker for PCs and iMovie for the Mac. You are now your own scriptwriter, director, and video producer. Next, take a topic from your content plan, pick a subject matter expert (you, someone in your office or a customer), find a good location, and shoot the video. Once it has been edited, you upload the video to YouTube. You can use the YouTube embedding code to add it to a blog article or use the link to share it on your social media sites.

The advantages of making it yourself are obviously the low cost. However, in my opinion, most businesses will pay a very high price for a low-cost video. It will potentially harm your brand if what you're creating looks like it was shot in your garage or in a spare office. There is a reason why most companies don't dare build their own website, and the same reason is true for corporate video. It pays to hire a design company to create the graphical look and feel, with the right design elegance, to tell your story on your website or on video. I strongly encourage you to do the same with your videos. You don't want your website or your video to look like it was the result of your daughter's or son's school project.

This is not true from every circumstance. In the Gary Vanerychuk example, he made his own videos and it worked for two main reasons; (1) because of the low cost he could produce lots of content and (2) the *content* was excellent. Another difference is Gary was marketing himself more than his dad's liquor store, to an audience that responds well to that style of content. If you are branding yourself, and your content is *really, really good*, then you can get away with poor video production quality. However, if you have a company brand and a customer who needs to trust the company more than the individual personalities, then homemade videos might not be a good choice.

The other disadvantage to making your video yourself is you are probably very good at your business but you might not be a great storyteller, director or video editor. Stick with what you do best and hire others to excel at what comes naturally to them. This would be the preferred way to represent your brand.

Professionally Produced Videos

If you work with a professional company, they'll bring in the highest quality equipment. At Splash Media, we take full advantage of our $5.5 million television studio to produce the best videos for our clients. With high-end equipment also comes high-end production staff, whose main purpose is to direct, shoot and edit company videos that are attractive, appealing and engaging.

If you're worried about the expense, you might be overestimating your investment. The going price for creating video today is approximately $1000 to $2000 for every one to two minutes of post-produced video content that's ready to be uploaded to YouTube. Therefore, if you are planning out your year and anticipate producing one video each month at $1000 to $2000 each, you are making a relatively small investment to tell your story and build your brand the right way. When you compare the investment to a TV commercial or even an ad in the paper that's here today and gone tomorrow, investing in TV-quality corporate videos that last forever and can be seen from virtually any Internet connected device can be one of the best marketing decisions you make.

The Tactical Wheel for YouTube

Listening

There are a few easy ways to listen as it relates to videos and YouTube. As I've mentioned, you can set up Google Alerts to filter just videos and then add that RSS feed to your iGoogle RSS Reader.

You can also pay attention to and post comments on other people's videos. YouTube has a new tool that they're Beta Testing as part of their TestTube, called CommentSearch, www.youtube.com/comment_search. You can do searches by key phrase and it will search through all the comments posted on YouTube. Then you can add to those comments and become part of the conversation. Remember, the purpose of listening is to identify conversations by potential customers and influencers who are involved in social media today.

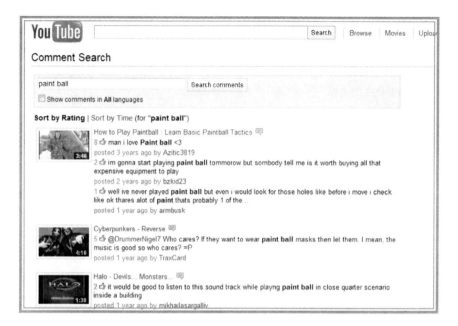

Another way to listen is to use your social media communities to ask and answer questions. You can send a broadcast message to your communities letting them know you want to create a video series to answer questions about your industry that are important to them. Ask for the three top burning questions, choose the responses you think are the most relevant, and then shoot videos to answer those questions.

Building Community

Building community is about getting people to friend and follow you; therefore, at the end of each video talk about your other social media channels and give them reasons why they might want to follow you. For instance, you can end the video with, "Be sure to follow us on Facebook where we share.....", or "Make sure you follow our blog, where you'll be able to see videos about....." Always tell your audience what's in it for them.

It's important to create your own free YouTube channel with

a custom background. Within the custom background cross-promote your other social media channels. Be sure to list your Facebook URL, any LinkedIn groups you might be a part of, how to get to your blog, and put your phone number or other pertinent information on your background.

In this example, Jordan Health Services is cross promoting their other social media environments with their custom background and within their video.

One of the best ways to build community is by making sure your videos are ranking well in the search engines. Remember, the *BusinessWeek* data showed that videos are 53 times more likely to show up in Google search results over websites, so do everything you can to make your video as search engine-friendly as possible.

One of the first things you can do is add the targeted key phrase that's related to the video in the file name. For the CRM software example I mentioned earlier, the key phrase was "What is CRM software." In this example, the filename should be what-is-crm-software.mp4. Because Google will look at the actual file name to determine what that particular digital item is about and your key phrases will give you a better opportunity to rank well.

You also want to add text titles and textual graphics in your videos. Google is now going to great lengths to understand what video is about, especially because they know the world is moving in that direction. Their bread-and-butter is all about providing relevant content, and so if customers would rather watch content than read it, they know they have to keep up with that trend. As of this writing, Google can't hear the words that are spoken in your video, but they can pick up any meta data you provide, as well as any overlay or titles you use to help them understand what that video is about.

In this example, having the targeted key phrase "What is CRM" within the video helps with video optimization.

> **3 Key Elements to Search Engine Optimize your Video**
>
> One of the points I made in the chapter on Search Engine Optimization is any electronic file has meta data, and meta data is just data about data. Within meta data there are critical areas where you'll drop clues for the search engines to understand what your videos are about, and these clues give you a good chance to rank well.
>
> **Title Tag:** Your title tag needs to be 60 or fewer characters, including the spaces, and should contain one or two targeted key phrases near the beginning. If you recall from the Search Engine Optimization chapter, search engines read prominence from left to right, so what you put toward the left of your title will be considered more important than what is on the right side.
>
> **Description Tag:** The description tag should be 500 or fewer characters, including spaces, and should reflect the video content while including the same one or two targeted key phrases.
>
> **Key Phrase Tags:** In the world of tagging, less is more. This is a big mistake that we see companies make. They try to tag for all their different key phrases but it's better to use only the really important key phrases, as it relates to the topic that's being covered in the video.

Broadcasting

You should publish your video to other sites beyond just YouTube, and there is a list of other important sites to consider in the Appendix of this book. Some of which you'll have to upload like you do at YouTube. For others, you'll just drop the RSS to the file to be included in their database or in their index.

Your broadcasting plan for your video should have several prongs:

1. **Summary blog:** Once you've uploaded a video on YouTube, write a summary as an article in your blog and

use the YouTube Player to view the video from the blog post. It's important to use the YouTube Player embed code as the way for the user to watch the video. You don't want the visitor to leave your blog and go to YouTube when they click on the video. You want that video to play from your blog because even though they're not on YouTube it will stream from YouTube and you'll get credit for that as a view on YouTube.

2. **Tweet blog link:** Once you have the permalink (specific URL) of your video summary blog and you've created a shortened URL, craft two to three tweets promoting the blog using different hashtags and rotating targeted key

phrases. Publish the tweets at different times throughout the month to drive traffic to your summary blog so your community will watch the video from your blog.

3. **Facebook update:** Post the video to Facebook as an update so it appears in the News Feed of your fans.

4. **Facebook Note:** Take the first couple of sentences of your video summary blog and make it a Facebook Note with a link to the blog summary of the video.

5. **LinkedIn:** If you add the video to your LinkedIn profile it will remain there for a long time. If you only want it to exist for a short period of time because it is tied to current events or a limited-time product, you can just post it as a status update on LinkedIn. Also use the video to start a discussion by posting it in your group and groups you belong to and ask other group members to share their opinions and feedback.

Developing Content

A good strategy for a small or medium size business is to commit to creating at least one video each month. While this is a lot less than what the largest companies in the world are doing, it will be enough for most companies to stay ahead of their competition while providing a steady diet of search engine-friendly video for their community. When it comes to your video content, you'll want to follow the same best practices that we've been covering throughout this entire book, where all the content you create is educational, leading with value, and designed to help your customer make good buying decisions.

If you ever get stuck trying to come up with ideas for video content, consider tapping into the following topics:

Successful YouTube Content:

Video FAQs - Ask your sales reps for the top five or six questions they hear most frequently and then produce a series of video FAQs that answer those questions.

Training – Teach your audience how to accomplish a task. In our case, we developed a series of "How To" videos for setting up and using various social media sites like Twitter and Facebook.

Facilities tour - Showing the behind-the-scenes happenings of your company, its inner workings and its culture does well on YouTube.

Video blog – Just like a normal blog, a video blog or Vlog is a chronological journal that uses video as the medium. Splash has a Vlog we call SplashCast (www.SplashMedia.com/resources/SplashCast). The articles are similar to those found in our blog, but they are videos in news-style format. Also, unlike SplashCast, this is the exception when it would be okay for you to use a flip-camera filming you at your desk talking about a quick topic.

Corporate overview – Tell and show your visitor what your company is about, including your vision and mission in a faster and more engaging format than they can read through on your website.

Product demonstrations and Instructional How-To's – Showing your customer how to use or assemble your product is a great opportunity for a video on YouTube.

Industry news – Provide a monthly summary of all the happenings within your industry via video. This is exceptionally powerful in the consultancy or services space.

Video case study/ success story/customer testimonials – Letting your best customers become your best salespeople by getting on camera and sharing how your company has helped them. Not only should you put customer testimonials on YouTube, but you should also include them on your website, and consider having your sales reps put the videos on an iPad or Tablet so they can play them for potential customers during the sales process.

You don't necessarily have to start from scratch when it comes to video content. Keep in mind that you might already have archived knowledge. Perhaps you already have video that's sitting on a shelf somewhere. Even if it's in VHS it can be converted over to digital. Does your company have any video that can be repurposed? You may have PowerPoint presentations or still images that you've shot in the past that can be coalesced together with a voice overlay and a soundtrack.

Conversion

It's important to use video to set yourself up for the conversion. When you're creating these videos, remember they can get shared and placed in other locations besides YouTube, so make sure you promote your company brand inside the videos. Include your company name and your contact information at the beginning and the end of your video, as well as on your YouTube custom background.

Use your videos to send people to your website or blog by promoting special offers and resources. For example, if you have an offer on your website to do a free analysis, create a video about it and direct people to your site for the analysis. Splash Media offers a free social media analysis on our website where people can give us information about what they're doing in the different social media environments, and we produce a report that shows them what their social media score is compared to all of our other clients. This analysis can be promoted by ending the video with, "To get a better understanding of what your social media score is, be sure to check out our website at splashmedia.com/resources and we'll conduct a free, no-cost social media analysis on your business."

I will close this chapter with a story that will help you understand why you need video and how just getting your line out in the water can catch all kinds of fish. I've already mentioned that we have a weekly vlog called SplashCast, but that's not all the videos we produce. We also have training videos, testimonial videos, as well as videos that highlight our culture. All of these can be found on YouTube. I want to focus on some videos we shot during the second half of 2010. At that time we were growing extremely fast and adding a couple of new team members each week. During the first week of employment at Splash, new team members are referred to as newbies while they go through our one-week training program. Back then, we introduced the newbies to the entire Splash team at our Friday morning staff meeting.

Since video is in our blood, we couldn't help ourselves and we started a video series that involved having all the newbies from a particular week compete in challenges we stole from the popular TV show *"Minute to Win It."* This is the game show where contestants compete in challenges using common household items like toilet paper, marbles, cups, etc. to win money. In our case the prize was $100. Typically the published video could be found on YouTube by that same afternoon.

I participated in one episode where each person had to strap a tissue box full of ping pong balls to their rear end like a backward fanny pack. We had to jump around and shake our rear ends to get as many balls out of the box as possible in one minute. I tried jumping, shaking, and rotating my posterior, but came up short. The videos are hilarious and are some of the most popular on our YouTube channel. After our first episode, we received a call from the producers of *"Minute to Win It,"* asking us if they could use our footage on their show. Obviously they were utilizing the social media marketing skill of *listening* to become aware of our videos in the first place. Of course we said yes, and since that time they have used two of our videos to promote their show.

It would be interesting enough if the story ended there. Around Christmas time, we ran out of fun games to play so we decided to make up our own "Minute To Win It" style game we called Reindeer Games that involved reindeer antlers and a cotton ball on a string.

Shortly after we published this video on YouTube, we were contacted by the producers again and they asked permission to use our game in their Christmas show! News also spread to the local NBC affiliate, who requested to come out and do a news story promoting the show, social media, and Splash Media. Of course we said yes, and because of using YouTube to create a window into our company and culture, we were now getting national and local TV coverage.

Anyone who learned about us from this exposure and went to our website to check us out would have learned about the Boot Camps I've mentioned in this book, as well as the free social media analysis. The following graph shows the increase in traffic to our website during this time, which also resulted in more conversions.

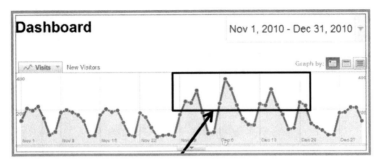

During December because of our local and national TV exposure from our YouTube videos, Splash's web traffic nearly doubled.

No other type of content has the reach and impact like video and leaving it out of your marketing strategy will limit your overall social media success. By adding videos you'll be able to tell your story and introduce your customers and prospects to your culture in a format that is in demand, accessible to just about any web-connected device (including television), and is relatively easy to produce.

Social Rules - YouTube:

Rule #57: Optimize your company's exposure by utilizing YouTube as the No. 2 search engine for your customers to find you.

Rule #58: Set up Google Alerts to notify you of videos published that target your key phrases so you can comment and/or share them with your followers.

Rule #59: Make sure your brand and contact information is clearly visible within each video, as well as within your custom YouTube background.

Rule #60: Place a call to action at the end of each video for people to connect with you on other social media platforms and to visit your website for more content and special offers.

Rule #61: Maximize your SEO results by creating effective File Names, Title Tags, Description Tags and Key Phrase Tags for your videos.

Rule #62: Create summary blogs posts about your YouTube channel videos and embed the video directly into the blog so your visitors do not leave your site to watch the video.

Rule #63: Share your videos in all other social media environments with a traceable bit.ly link.

16. BLOGS

This may be the most important chapter in the book. We have spent a lot of time talking about why social media is a revolution, how to build a successful strategy for your business, and we've covered all of the major platforms in detail. However, if you don't master the revolution and leverage the major platforms to draw visitors to your blog, your success will be limited. All roads should point to a blog that you own, manage and control - period.

What is a blog? I'm sure there's a lot of business owners who've heard the terms blog and blogging and have really not understood what they mean. I'm guessing there are many people who have read a blog without even realizing it. In the context of this book, a blog is just another web presence for a business. Your corporate blog is like your corporate journal that needs to be updated on a regular basis.

Unlike a personal journal, the purpose of a corporate blog is to benefit others. It's a journal you're creating to help other people, typically your customers, potential customers, stakeholders, and partners. Information is what your target audience is seeking. Information gives your followers knowledge, and that knowledge empowers them to make purchasing decisions with confidence. Status updates, tweets, and posts are limited in their ability to deliver knowledge. They are lures to ultimately drive people to your blog. A blog is the best way to create compelling content that empowers users while connecting them to your company. Along with potential and existing customers, search engines will devour your fresh blog content and reward you with good rankings on their sites. Some people will go so far as to say "blog" is an acronym for Better Listings on Google. Although the acronym is not true, the connection between blogs and rankings is accurate.

One of the key ingredients of social media success is dialogue, which means your blog shouldn't be a one-way conversation in which you're pushing content out to your followers. Readers expect to participate and you should encourage them to engage in the conversation. Also, the responsibility of blogging should not be on just one person within your company. Look to subject matter experts within your organization and potentially external experts to create consistent content for your blogs.

You might be thinking you already have a website, so why do you need a blog? There are some significant advantages a blog has over your website in the world of social media and Internet marketing today. Your website is like an online brochure. It's telling the story and history of your company, as well as providing information about the products and services you provide. Hopefully it's telling visitors what makes your company unique, but in the end your website is relatively static and finite.

When you created your website it was probably similar to the process you went through to have a brochure developed. You sat down and thought about what you're trying to communicate, you wrote content for every page and you didn't approve it until everything was perfect. The end product was a finite communication tool. The big difference with a blog is it's a living organism; it's always growing. It's also where community is building in an environment you completely control. You have less control over every other environment we've talked about thus far. However, your blog gives you ultimate and total control. Your blog is where the culture and personality of your company will shine, and where you'll provide enticing offers for your followers to learn more about and engage deeper with your company. Your website content tends to be more formal and your blog is more business casual or even completely casual depending on your company culture and image. Your blog will become the most important environment you maintain for your social media strategy. In fact, your blog needs to become the hub of the entire process. If you look at the following chart, the purpose of every other social media platform (Twitter, Facebook, LinkedIn, YouTube, etc.) is to drive traffic from those sites to your blog and website. Your blog is the hub of it all, and that's where you're telling your story and giving people the opportunity to engage with you at a deeper level.

Why your blog should be the central command of your social media strategy:

The blog gives you total control of content that has a long shelf life. What do you think the shelf life is of a tweet? A few minutes? A day or two at most? The same is true for the shelf life of a post on your Facebook wall or profile. However, the shelf life of an article on your blog is basically forever. Search engines and users alike can access articles months and years after they've been written.

Blog acts as the primary website for SEO. Your blog has webpages just like your website does, and to Google they are more relevant than any page on your site. When you create an article and put it in your blog, Google will crawl the page, add it to their database, and index it just like any page in your website. What that means is you can write an article today on a particular topic and two or three years from now, a potential customer could do a search for that topic and your blog will appear in the search rankings and they can access the article directly from the search engine. Because of the real-time nature of the other social media platforms, tweets, Facebook posts, and LinkedIn status updates won't appear in search results over time.

Best place for SEO because you control clues. We spent a lot of time covering this in the SEO 2.0 chapter, but as a reminder, you're able to provide clues for the search engines to help them clearly understand what all of your blog pages are about. This gives you a better opportunity to rank well for important key phrases, more so than your website and certainly over the other social media platforms.

Great place for generating conversions. It's hard to tell your story or add a conversion form on a platform like Twitter or Facebook. With Twitter you only have 140 characters and that includes any links. The beautiful thing about a blog is you can put a form on a blog just like a website. You can put your toll-free number on your blog, just like your website. You can put offers to download premium content like e-books and white papers on your blog. You can even have event registration right in your blog post. It's a great place for converting browsers into buyers.

Take a look at the following chart. It drives home the concept that your blog is a living, breathing organism that can generate a lot of opportunities for your business. I call this growth curve a hockey stick because once you get to this critical mass of more than 50 blogs of great content and consistent engagement from your community, the conversions you should expect to generate through social media will skyrocket.

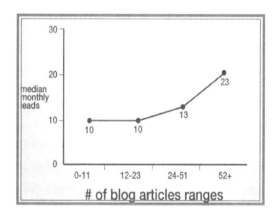

Purpose of your blog

Educate your target audience about your industry. You are the expert, you know more about your industry than customers and potential customers do, and the best way to earn their business is to be informative. For example, one of the purposes of the Splash Media blog is to be a social media industry news source for business owners. During a typical week, Renay San Miguel, our Chief Content Officer, will post two or three journalistic-style articles about what's going on within the industry. He researches breaking news, attends industry events, and interviews social media managers of large companies to write articles that inform our followers. We know when business owners become interested in social media they'll start looking for information to get educated and up-to-speed, and we want to be a resource for them.

Help potential customers formulate their buying criteria. Going back to the Universal Marketing Funnel we covered in the Content chapter, one of the critical stages is the Evaluation phase. This is when people are researching to learn about all of the options available to them and formulating their buying criteria. Your blog can educate and help them understand the pros and cons of the different options available so they can make an informed buying decision. Articles such as "10 Questions to Ask Before You Purchase Your Next Car" or "Cloud-based vs. Desktop Accounting Software: Who wins?" will be consumed by prospects that are in the Evaluation stage.

Promote your partners and vendors. Your business exists inside an ecosystem and it is successful not only because of the products and services you provide, but also because of people you help and those who help you. Help your partners and vendors by giving them access and exposure to your target audience by including articles about how working with them helps you provide better solutions for your customers. In exchange for your effort, you want your partners and vendors to talk about you in their blogs.

Promote your products and services. Create content for your blogs that talk about the benefits your customers enjoy as a result of using your products and services. Interviewing happy customers to produce case studies or success stories are excellent ways to feature your products and services.

Provide a glimpse into the people and the culture of your company. Your blog is an opportunity for you to let your hair down a little bit and let people see and connect with you on a personal level. Remember, people do business with people. Your blog is a great opportunity to create a personal connection with your target audience, and one of the best ways to do that is to let the culture, your personality and the different people in your company shine through in your blog. For example, Splash Media had a blog series, titled "Tales from the Road," which featured weekly stories about our experiences while we were on the road delivering boot camps across the country. This gave us the opportunity to share our company culture, highlight some of the Splash Media team, and also promote our events.

The Power of RSS

RSS, which stands for Really Simply Syndication, is the fuel that sparks the fire in getting your blog out into the world and helping you stay in touch with the followers of your blog. RSS is like a beacon that emits from your blog whenever anything new is added. When readers click on the RSS subscribe button they will be automatically notified when anything new is added. This is a great feature because rather than hoping someone comes back to your blog every few days, they are notified that something new is available and this gives them a reason to come back. If fact, they can even read your new article from their RSS reader without having to visit your site at all.

Through RSS your blog will actually show up right inside their reader (Google Reader, BlogNavigator, NewsGator, etc.) This is a great efficiency tool because there's so much content online that anyone could surf for hours and days and not remember where they found a particular article. By using the RSS feed to your blog, your visitors will be constantly linked to you and be notified of new content on your site.

Examples of Successful Company Blogs

In order to give you a sense of what a vibrant, healthy corporate blog looks like, take a look at some of my favorites.

37 Signals is a software company most known for their widely used web-based project management platform called Base Camp. They've also written a great book titled *Rework*, which is a summation of many of the articles written for their two blogs. Their company blog, Signal vs. Noise, provides insight about their products, business, design, editorial, and other topics. I

encourage you to take a look and get a sense of the way they're building community and the types of content they're creating.

Another great example of how a very large organization can let the culture and personality of their company shine through is the **Southwest Airlines** blog. Southwest Airlines is an amazing company. When you consider the major difficulties the airline industry has had over the past couple of decades, it's hard to believe Southwest Airlines continues to pull a profit over and over again. Even though they treat us all like cattle, they do it with a smile on their face. One of the key components to their success is they're a very human, approachable company. As you might imagine, their blog follows suit and does a great job at continuing to promote their corporate culture.

Safe Phace is another of Slash Media's clients, and they're doing a good job of using their blog to build community and offer insight into their industry while also selling their products.

For all of you small business owners out there who can't imagine how a blog would help your business or industry, check out **ElectricMan.** He is the epitome of the small business man, using a very vibrant blog that does a great job of providing advice to homeowners and businesses about wiring, emergency power, and general maintenance. His blog has become a great source of leads for new business. You may remember the case study mentioned in Chapter 8 (Building Community) about how ElectricMan's blog generated a great deal of business from the Red Cross.

Blog Platform Recommendations

There are a lot of different blog platforms available to you, such as Tumblr, Typepad, and Live Journal, but my recommendation is to use WordPress for ease of administration. WordPress is a blogging format you add to your existing website or you can build your entire website on a WordPress platform. Normally it's free or very little cost for your web host provider to add WordPress to your website.

Advantages to using WordPress:

1. WordPress has a great content management system that really makes it rookie-proof to manage and administer for people who don't understand the technology (HTML code and programming) to get in the game and start adding blog content without a huge learning curve.

2. There are lots of great plug-ins (added features and applications) for WordPress that'll make your life easier and will help you promote your blog online. The following list includes plug-ins that we have vetted at Splash Media and use for our clients.

    - All-in-One SEO Pack – makes it easy to optimize blog posts for search engines.

    - Google Analyticator - enables Google Analytics logging on any WordPress blog.

    - Google XML Sitemaps with multi-site support – automatically adds blog articles to your Google XML site map.

    - Twitter for WordPress – displays your tweets on your blog.

    - WordPress.com Stats - additional analytics.

    - WPtouch - adds CSS (Cascading Style Sheet) for viewing on mobile devices.

- WP Buttons – adds share buttons to your blog that allows visitors to easily share your posts.

The Tactical Wheel for Blogging

Listening

How do you engage in listening through a blog? There are two primary ways to listen. One is by paying attention to the comments people make and any reposting or linking back to your blog. If you follow the strategy laid out in this book, other people will begin sharing your content. One of the best ways to know when people are referencing you is to set up a Google Alert that sends you an email daily or weekly that references each time your company name or variations of your company name appears online in blogs, articles and Twitter. Also, make sure your blog is set up to notify you of backlinks, which is anytime someone links to your individual blog URL.

The second way to listen is to set up a Google Alert around important key phrases and select Blog as the content type. This will keep you abreast of relevant blog articles, and you can decide if you want to contribute to the conversation by commenting.

Building Community

Building community from your blog is a little different than from the other platforms. Remember, all roads lead to your blog and the primary goal of the other platforms is to build community, broadcast useful content, and draw your followers to your blog. Here are a few ways to build community and readership:

1. Enable the RSS feature on your blog by having a button to make it very easy for your visitors to subscribe.

2. Include links to your other social media environments. This is easily done with the free WordPress plug-ins mentioned earlier. These plug-ins provide you with very visible buttons on every page of your blog that read, "Follow us on Twitter," "Follow us on Facebook," "Follow us on LinkedIn." Also use the Bookmark plug-in that allows your readers to easily repost and share every blog with their community with just one click of Tweet This, Like This, Share This, etc.

3. Use your blog as a clearinghouse for promotions you might run in other social media environments. As mentioned in previous chapters, use your blog as a landing page to explain the details about promotions and special offers.

Broadcasting

Remember when you're promoting blog content or broadcasting anything, follow the 90/10 rule. If 100% of what you're promoting inside these social media channels is just your blog content, people will quickly tune you out. Here's how to broadcast your blog across your other social media platforms.

Twitter: Use the headline of the blog, along with a keyword-rich hashtag and a Bit.ly link to easily direct people to your blog. When you are writing your headline of the blog, be mindful of popular hashtags relevant to your topic. Use Bit.ly to monitor the traffic of when, who and how often the shortened URL is being accessed. Plan on tweeting at least two to three times about each blog and spread them out over the course of a week.

Facebook: Post a summary of each blog on your wall and ask for feedback. Use the Notes feature in Facebook to create a teaser summary of the blog that allows people to click on a link to read the full article

Above: Promoting a blog article on Facebook wall and using a poll tied to the article to generate engagement.

Below: Facebook note with link to the blog article.

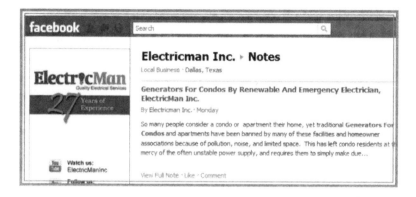

LinkedIn: You can easily set up the BlogLink feature within your LinkedIn profile so each blog is automatically streamed to both your personal profile and company profile and looks like a new status update on your page. By doing this, your blog will show up within the LinkedIn Update emails your connections receive periodically. As discussed in the LinkedIn chapter post your blog in your group and solicit feedback; also post it in the different groups in which you are a member.

Here is an example of how broadcasting your blog in these environments can generate engagement and leads as well as build awareness. Victory Energy is a Splash Media client who manufactures and maintains industrial boilers. Following the methods outlined in this chapter, we were broadcasting a blog series on boiler maintenance. The blog articles were placed in Facebook notes, as Facebook wall posts, published within approximately 20 LinkedIn groups and tweeted multiple times on Twitter. A plant operations manager who was following us on Twitter re-tweeted one of our posts, which meant everyone following the plant manager was now exposed to our content. We responded by thanking him and asking him for his opinion about

Victory's blog. He told us he visits the blog every day and uses our tips in his operations with his team. We went into LinkedIn, searched for his profile and learned he shared a common group with Victory's VP of Sales and made the connection. Now Victory could reach out and follow up with the plant manager to discuss their needs.

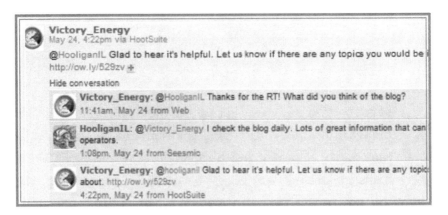

Developing Content

This is the crossroads where your social media marketing activities will either succeed or fail. You can expend lots of energy doing all the items recommended in this book to build community, engage your audience, and draw them to your blog, but if your content (how do I say this nicely……sorry, I can't think of a better way) sucks, then it will all be for naught. Imagine how disappointed your fans will be when you tease them with the lure of great information, they take the bait and land on your blog and discover their 6-year old, first-grader could have written a better post with more useful information. I challenge you to produce *remarkable* content; content that your users will read and share with their colleagues. With remarkable content you both win.

Blog Article Best Practices

Obviously your blog is the critical component of creating content because it's the clearinghouse for all of your content. At a minimum write at least one new blog post each week. Remember the Universal Marketing Funnel and create content for each stage according to your content plan. This will ensure you are speaking to all of your readers, regardless of where they are in the buying process. Here are some other best practices to consider:

1. **Summarize your videos.** Even when you create a video for YouTube you should create an article in your blog that summarizes the video, and then embed the video directly into the blog.

2. **Curate other people's content.** There will always be other influencers and stakeholders in your industry who will have relevant and informative things to say, and you'll want your followers to have access to that information. Writing a summary of that information and linking to the original content helps you make things easy for your potential customers to learn and better understand your industry. When you curate other people's content, be sure to include a direct link to the original author's blog or website so your audience can read the full story on the author's site. Your summary or abstract of the content is what gets people to your blog first.

3. **Ask open-ended questions to get the dialogue going.** You want comments on your blogs. Ask people for their opinions to get them sharing their thoughts.

4. **Write controversial posts.** Take a stand with your blog content and don't be afraid to share your opinion.

5. **Connect with current events.** Tie in your expertise with current events and create blog articles about your suggestions, opinions, and responses to those events.

Conversion

Just like your blog is the clearinghouse for all of your content, it should also be the clearinghouse for deeper engagement opportunities. Your blog should include both passive and active calls to action. A passive call to action is simply having a toll-free number sitting on your blog if readers decide they want to call or ask questions. You're not encouraging them or telling them to call, but you're making it easy for them to connect with you if a want or need arises. An active call to action is when you're actually encouraging them and selling them on why they should take the next step. You can easily promote calls to action in the left or right column of your blog. This way they're always visible and present to your readers. In the following example, the Splash Media blog uses the right column to promote offers for deeper engagement that includes a free social media analysis.

The Splash Media Blog offers four calls to action; register for boot camp, follow us, sign up for automatic updates, and to receive a free social media analysis.

You can also promote calls to action within the body of specific blog posts. On every evaluation and decision blog article you publish, include an active call to action that's closely related to that article. Perhaps you've created a white paper on a particular topic in which you are discussing the pros and cons of different types of features about a product you've described in your blog. Make it easy for readers to take that next step by providing a link for them to download your free PDF. Maybe you have a decision piece and you're a B2B company and you want to offer a buyer's kit to the reader. At the end of the content you might say, "By the way, we've created a buyer's kit to help companies think through and formulate how to get a project like this passed through the purchasing department within their organization. Click here to access your free buyer's kit." In each case you request an email address to gain access to the free download, which will help you build your contacts list.

I encourage you to come back to this chapter often and become a master blogger. All roads should point to your blog, and developing fresh, remarkable content your visitors read and share is *the* key for social media marketing success. If done correctly, your blog can outperform your website in traffic and conversions. Good luck!

Social Rules - Blog:

Rule #64: Your blog is the No. 1 social media marketing platform. All other platforms should be used to build community and drive traffic to your blog.

Rule #65: Use your blog as a way to increase SEO, provide valuable information to your potential customers and promote your products.

Rule #66: Listen to comments made on your blog, and set up Google Alerts to notify you anytime your company name or targeted key phrases appear in other blogs, so you can jump in on those conversations.

Rule #67: Build your community by setting up an RSS feed so people can easily subscribe to your blog.

Rule #68: Integrate Follow Us buttons on every page of your blog so your community can become followers on other platforms.

Rule #69: Add share button plug-ins so your readers can expose your blog content to their followers.

Rule #70: Broadcast your blog content and drive traffic to your blog by posting headlines and links on Twitter, Facebook and LinkedIn.

Rule #71: Create value-added content for your readership and also curate other people's content within your blog for a stronger following.

Rule #72: Integrate passive and active calls to action within your blog to maximize engagement.

17. MEASURING RESULTS

Just like with any other type of marketing activity you should be measuring your social media marketing efforts. The one challenge with social media is there are elements that are more difficult to measure than the other types of marketing activities you might have been involved with in the past. For example, you can run an ad in the newspaper on Sunday and get immediate response which will give you a sense of how well the ad performed. That's the benefit of this type of marketing activity. Unfortunately, most advertising has a very short shelf life. It's like renting a hotel room. As long as you pay, you can stay. However, expending effort to build a fully engaged community in social media is like building a house. You'll be able to enjoy the benefits of your efforts forever.

Just like building a house, it's a slower process so the lead time between your efforts and results is longer, if your only measuring stick is sales. With social media marketing there's a lot more going on between you and your potential customers because you're leading with value and building relationships first. This is not a requirement in the traditional marketing world in which you're only attracting *now* buyers. In fact, it's not even possible to nurture relationships and lead with value. Social media marketing is different.

Once you're working to build awareness about your business people will begin to recognize you as a thought leader, but you still won't know what direct influence that has on a potential customer. What may very well happen with social media is somebody could become aware of your company based on one of their friends liking your content on Facebook and it shows up on their News Feed. That same person could be doing research on Google a few weeks later and see a blog article you've written show up in their search results. They could read the article but still not take any action. A few days could pass and they're on Twitter and see a tweet you posted, which lands them to your Facebook page, where they decide to like your page and become part of your community. Now your Facebook posts start to show up on their News Feed. It could be another six months later before they've finally been convinced to take action based on the value of the content they received from your various environments. When they do decide to take action, they might simply walk into your location or they may pick up the phone and call you.

Don't get discouraged by the length of this scenario. As I've been saying throughout this entire book, social media is about building community—not getting right to the sale. So how do you measure all of this effort? There are both macro and micro ways to measure your progress, but the purpose behind measuring is always the same. You want to ensure your efforts are lining up with your overall strategic plan. You want to create a roadmap that tells you how you're going to get from point A to point Z, and measuring gives you the ability to see where you are in that process.

As you develop a strategy and identify what that roadmap looks like and you begin to measure your progress, you'll be able to tell where you are doing well and manage by exception those places where you can improve. This will prevent you from becoming too myopic and focused in on areas that don't need your attention, as well as provide a sense of direction early on as your efforts are being invested without a lot of return in the form of sales. As we go through this chapter we'll look at how to measure in four different ways, macro, micro, comparative, as well as, how to measure by platform based on the Tactical Wheel.

Macro Measuring

When you think about macro measuring, consider when Nike sponsored Michael Jordan to wear and promote their products. How do they know if they're getting a good return? How do they measure that investment and effort? This is similar to getting your arms around measuring the return on investment on things like new sales collateral for your sales reps or fancy new office furniture to impress customers, or putting a coffee shop in your car dealership. The same is true for the macro side of social media marketing. How do you know if your investment in social media is working? These are harder things to measure, but they *should* be measured and they *can* be measured.

The number one thing you need to measure over time is the bottom line. At the end of the day social media marketing has the word "marketing" in it and that is all about driving people toward your brand and eventually benefiting your business as you deliver a value to your consumers. You want to see your bottom line improve over time. Remember the hierarchy of needs. Profit is at the top of the pyramid. In the Strategy chapter, we discussed how improved profits should be a goal of your social media marketing efforts, but that the stages at the top took longer to achieve.

Social media marketing is not about starting to engage and then seeing a huge increase in profits 30 days from now—or even six months from now. It's more important and more realistic to compare how you are doing after a year of being fully engaged. You are building a house, not renting a hotel room.

Moving down from the profit stage on the pyramid, another macro component you can measure is lift in overall sales. Are you selling more today than you were before you engaged in social media marketing? The same applies with your leads; are you generating more qualified leads today? Are you getting more phone calls or walk-ins as a result of social media marketing?

When you do look at these macro elements, everything else

should be held constant. For instance, if you compare your bottom line this year to that of last year as it relates to social media, that should be the only component you change in your marketing plan. Otherwise, you won't know if the increase or decrease is a result of social media engagement or the fact that you made some other change like taking trade shows off of your marketing schedule. You won't be able to do a fair macro analysis because there are too many factors that can affect and skew your data. By only adding one new element like social media, you'll be able to better measure your results.

Micro Measuring

Measuring micro elements will help you analyze the road you are on to drive you toward macro results. Because social media marketing has long lead times between effort and results, every business must measure a sub-set of these micro elements I will be presenting throughout the rest of this chapter. I've broken down the micro piece into multiple sections, so we'll look at what to measure by platform and then we'll measure progress as we're getting a campaign up and running. Finally, we'll measure based on the Tactical Wheel.

It's really important when you decide on these micro elements that you start by taking a baseline analysis or snapshot of where you are so you can measure how well you're doing from the get-go and then over time.

Comparative Analysis

Along with macro and micro measuring, you'll also want to

get a sense of how the results of your social media efforts are comparing to the rest of the world. At Splash Media, we found comparative analysis to be critical for the success of our clients. Benchmarking our clients against other B2B or B2C companies' social media environments we felt were best in class helps us clearly see where we need to go to help our clients also become best in class. SplashCube is the tool we use for our clients. SplashCube uses complex algorithms to analyze hundreds of thousands of environments to measure and grade each one against four factors:

1. Frequency: How often companies post within their social media profiles.

2. Broadcasting: How often users comment on broadcasted posts.

3. Interest: How often their posts are shared outside of their communities.

4. Outreach: How active they are in creating new relationships and conversations.

SplashCube compares companies' social media profiles and grades them according to frequency, broadcasting, interest, and outreach.

This helps us take any subjectivity out of our actions and gives us a way to benchmark our clients against the best in class social media profiles. Other than SplashCube, you can check out your competitors' environments and document how many followers they have and how often they broadcast. You can then compare this over time and see how you are stacking up.

Website

The first thing that we'll look at is your website. As we discussed in the Strategy chapter, you should expect the number of unique visitors coming to your website to increase across the board. Because people may type your website address in their browser, click directly to your site through social media, or find your site by doing a Google search, you'll want to measure the overall increase in unique visitors over time. Other important website elements include:

Visitors by source. For instance, how many visitors are you getting from search engines, your blog, Facebook, LinkedIn, YouTube, and Twitter?

Inbound links. As people share your content and posts, links to your website should increase over time. You can measure this at Google by typing in this command-- Link:www.yourcompany.com.

Website conversions. You also want to measure the number of conversions by source. For instance, how many people are registering for your events, requesting quotes, signing up to get your e-book or white paper? Of all your social traffic, 3% to 5% should opt-in to something on your website.

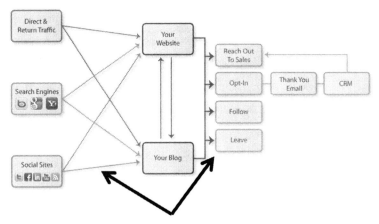

Traffic to your website and blog should increase over time across all sources. Conversions should also increase as traffic grows and you tweak your calls to action.

Blog

Like your website, you want to see how many visitors are actually coming to your blog, over time and by source. However, one of the unique elements of your blog to track is how often your articles are being mentioned inside of other people's social media environments or on the Internet in general. It's easy to add a plug-in to your website that allows readers to quickly share your content on Twitter and Facebook. This will also make it easy for you to see how often the content was shared directly from your blog.

Using Word Press plug-ins like WP Buttons recommended in the Blog chapter make it easy to see how many people share your blog content.

Along with your website, measure the number of conversions from your blog, as well as conversions that are happening through blog comments, re-tweets and Facebook shares. Think of your blog as a secondary website and measure how many leads your blog is getting and how it is contributing to your overall pipeline.

Most website analytics tools will be able to provide this information for both your website and blog. Google Analytics is the analytics tool we use for our Splash Media clients, but you might also consider Hitslink, Webtrends, or SiteCatalyst. Each of these tools provides the data you need to measure your progress.

Twitter

With Twitter, look at and measure the increase of followers over time. Also measure the number of re-tweets or re-posts of what you're broadcasting out through Twitter. By using a free shortened URL service like Bit.ly you can track and measure the number of clicks your blog and website links are getting through Twitter and Facebook posts, and even see which platform is producing the most traffic.

Facebook

With Facebook, measure the increase in the number of people liking your Facebook page over time. Also measure comments posted on your Facebook page. By monitoring the comments made by your community you'll learn what types of broadcasts engage your audience better than others, and then you can hone in on the success and broadcast in a voice that is more palatable to your followers so they will engage with you more often. Through Facebook you have the opportunity to run contests, sweepstakes and conduct polls and surveys, so measure the performance of those activities as well. Start with a desired outcome like 200 new fans, or 100 visits to your website, or 20 new leads. You'll want to know the results from these campaigns so you can learn from them and improve your effectiveness.

Facebook Insights is a monitoring tool available inside the administration section of your company page. Beyond monitoring likes, you can also monitor impressions, and post feedback over time. You'll want to see these numbers increase over time.

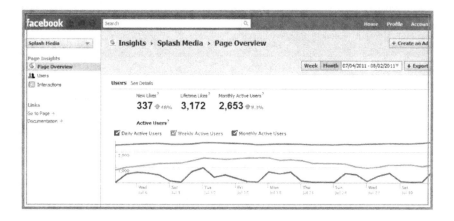

LinkedIn

Within LinkedIn, measure the number of personal connections you have within your network. Set a goal for the number of new connections you want to add each month and then measure against that goal. A typical business owner should be able to add 30-50 new connections each month. Also measure the number of members of your LinkedIn group. LinkedIn offers good information about how users interact with your company profile. You can monitor the number of people following your company page, the amount of traffic, and page views over time.

YouTube

Like Facebook and LinkedIn, YouTube provides data about viewer engagement. Within your channel, under the Insight tab, you can learn how many times your videos have been viewed, the demographics of your viewers, and where they came from. Within YouTube you can measure the total number of views for all of your videos, as well as the number of views per video. If you want to measure conversions from your videos, consider promoting a conversion page on your website that is only accessible to users by typing in the URL. Promote the URL link in your videos by telling viewers to go to that page for additional information. For instance, at the end of the video you could say "For more information about how CRM Software can help your business grow, visit yourwebsite.com/YouTube." This will enable you to track the number of people who go to this page and convert into leads or sales.

Stages of Measurement

Let's switch gears and talk about measuring success over time because you need to have proper expectations about results and you don't want to hold your social media activities accountable to the same measuring stick at every stage of maturity. There are three stages of a social media campaign—the crawling stage, the walking stage and the running stage—and you want to use different measuring sticks at different times because your needs are different for each stage.

Earlier, I explained how you should learn how to crawl before you walk and walk before you run when it comes to learning and engaging in social media. Let's take a look at measuring success using that same analogy.

Crawling Stage

The crawling stage of measurement is the first three months. The most important thing to measure from Day One to the end of month three is your growth in community. You don't want to be too wrapped up in traffic flow, leads or conversions. You just want to focus on increasing your Twitter followers, growing you connections and increasing your group members in LinkedIn, and getting more Facebook likes.

The other thing to measure in your first three months is your activity goals because it's important to build good habits that will allow you to succeed down the road. Hold yourself accountable and make sure you're hitting your strategy and delivering the right frequency of blogs, Facebook posts, Twitter broadcasts, LinkedIn status updates and YouTube videos. Once you've held yourself accountable for three months you should be in a good rhythm. At the end of the first three months you should be able to look back and see at least 12 blog posts, two to three videos published, and 50 or more Tweets and Facebook posts. You will also want to complete the six-step activation process outlined in the Building Community chapter.

Walking Stage

In months four through six, you will start measuring your results. Not only will you continue to measure the same things you did in the crawling stage but you also want to measure new elements. Start measuring engagement such as increases in the number of re-posts or re-tweets, Facebook shares and likes registered on your status updates. You want to start to see more activity with regard to the number of mentions of your business and people sharing your content.

Also pay attention to community growth. During this stage, you want your Twitter and Facebook followers and LinkedIn connections to grow by a net of 20% over the previous month. Some people will connect with you while a small percentage may disconnect, but the net increase should be at least 20%. It is perfectly okay to have people decide you might not be a good fit for them and vice-versa. Ultimately you're trying to build a community of people who are congruent with your brand and your unique selling and value propositions.

You also want to see your Twitter follower-to-following ratio shift. In the crawling stage you will be a bit upside down, meaning you'll be following more people (perhaps 50% -100% more) than are following you, but eventually you want to see that ratio of following-to-followers decline over time.

Since your focus is shifting from building community to engaging your community, this is also a good time to begin measuring the number of visitors (clicks) on the URL links you are sharing with your community, as well as the amount of views you're getting on your YouTube videos. During this walking stage, start measuring your search engine rankings for targeted key phrases. For instance, go into Google, do a search for a key phrase or type in a topic of a blog that you generated and see your blog show up on the first couple pages of Google. In addition, measure traffic to your website and blog based on search engine traffic and referral traffic.

Running Stage

From month seven and beyond you are in the running stage of measuring results and you'll want to add conversions to your measuring stick during this stage. You want to start looking at how many leads, phone calls, walk-ins and redeemed coupons you're generating from the different social media sources. You also want to start looking at your costs-per-action, cost-per-lead or cost-per-acquisition compared to the target objective you set out for social media. It's okay to look at these elements during the first six months, but you don't want to pay too much attention until month seven. This is when you'll have enough data to make some intelligent decisions on how to best tweak your strategy to optimize results.

At this stage, a typical business should have at least 500 Facebook Fans and Twitter followers. However this is not a hard-and-fast rule, as each business is different and has a different customer base. Also, your Twitter follower-to-following ratio should be getting closer to one-to-one, meaning you have the same number of followers (or more) than you are following. This is also the point when you want to see your communities start taking on a life of their own. For instance, you should see people using your Facebook page to connect for customer service issues or endorsing and praising your company. People should be reaching out to you on Twitter, @tagging or replying to you. You should be spending time each day responding to comments or questions via your social media accounts. If these things are not happening by the seventh month, there's probably something wrong with the type of content you're publishing and posting through social media.

The Tactical Wheel for Measuring Results

Listening

You know you're doing an effective job of listening if you're finding people to connect and engage with on a regular basis. Opportunities should be presenting themselves for you to either connect or actually reach out to and help people that you've identified in Facebook, Twitter, etc. Also your number of followers should be increasing every week because you are listening to and finding influencers and customers. As a general rule, you should be identifying and following 20 to 40 new *qualified, relevant influencers* and *potential customers* each month. The way you find them is by listening, not by simply following anyone you see.

Building Community

The number one way you measure building community is by how many fans, followers and connections you have on your various social media platforms. These numbers should increase by 20% month after month until you reach the running stage. At the running stage you will need to come up with new growth goals that are appropriate for your business. For example, once we hit 2000 likes on the Splash Media Facebook page, growing by 20% was unrealistic. We are now happy with 7% net growth each month. Conversely, we have greater expectations for our LinkedIn group because we invite users who attend our Social Media for CEOs Boot Camps to our group. Each month we have about 1000 people attend the boot camps and we expect a high percentage of them to join our group, so our growth goals in LinkedIn haven't tapered down.

Broadcasting

The way you measure the success of broadcasting is the number of reposts, comments, and likes you get whenever you broadcast information. You can also measure the amount of inbound traffic to your site or your blog; remember, broadcasting is like fishing to get people to go somewhere else, namely your blog or website. The number of clicks you're getting on your links indicates how well you are doing with broadcasting relevant and useful content.

Developing Content

The impact of the social media content you create for your target audience to consume, such as blogs and videos, can also be measured. Take a look at the number of likes, tweets or shares on a particular item, and the number of page views (how many people actually look at that piece of content). If you have a call to action in your blog, for example, you can see if you are generating conversions based on that content. You'll also want to measure search results and search engine traffic as an indicator of how well your content is working for you.

Conversion

The last piece of the Tactical Wheel is about generating some type of measurable action taken by your target audience. Of course, this will be the easiest to measure and the most valuable for your business when your social media strategy is mature and humming along. You'll want to measure conversion rates, total number of leads/opt-ins by source, such as blogs, Twitter, and Facebook. Also measure the total number of sales/walk-ins by source, as well as the number of registrations for events by source. Take your cost-per-conversion and compare this to your goal and against other advertising and marketing sources. This is calculated by adding up hard (advertising dollars) and soft (your time) costs and dividing this by your conversions. If your cost-per-conversion for social media is lower than your other marketing methods, then you have hit the top of the hierarchy of the needs pyramid; profit.

By using the techniques outlined in this chapter, you'll be able to make good decisions and continual tweaks to your campaigns and strategies to optimize performance. Once you have, then your goal should be to continue to refine your efforts to lower your cost per conversions, which will increase profit. Every dollar you save will drop to your bottom line.

Social Rules - Measuring Results:

Rule #73:   Measuring results in social media is different than traditional media because there is a lot more going on between your community and your brand. Therefore, you will need to measure more than conversions.

Rule #74:   Consider the hierarchy of needs and identify measurable goals for each stage. Conduct a comparative analysis to benchmark your company against top competitors.

Rule #75   Traffic to your website and blog should increase from all sources over time.

Rule #76:   Use bit.ly to monitor the traffic by volume and by source to your blog and videos. Also use social media plug-ins within your content to see how often articles are shared.

Rule #77   Remember the three stages of maturity for social media marketing efforts: crawling, walking, and running. Develop realistic goals for each stage.

18. TYING IT ALL TOGETHER

It's time to start leveraging the Tactical Wheel to maximize your efforts for each social media platform. I am confident that, if you focus your energies on the platforms and best practices outlined in this book, you will be in a good position to optimize social media marketing for your business. Let me leave you with some key next steps and final thoughts.

As soon as you put this book down

Take action. Don't think for a minute the revolution we find ourselves in is going away anytime soon. Consumers will not suddenly stop using social media. They will continue to leverage the power it has given them to communicate to their friends their likes, dislikes and opinions related to your products or services.

Start thinking about how you can influence more than sell your product and what you can do to get people talking about you by empowering them and giving them a voice. Consider ways you can lead with value by becoming a social media concierge for your customers and prospects. Also begin to determine what types of social media currency will benefit your followers.

Go to the resources section of the Splash Media website and watch the videos on key phrase research and content planning. Download the questionnaire and purpose-by-platform worksheet so you can start building your Social Media Business Plan. Check out what your competitors are doing and document key metrics you plan to use to monitor your progress. Finally, make a list of internal and external resources you'll need to succeed. For example, choose subject matter experts to help with developing content and a community manager to listen, monitor, and engage with your communities in Facebook, LinkedIn, and Twitter. From an external resource perspective, consider the tools you'll need to use like TweetDeck, HootSuite, or SplashCube, as well as what parts of the process you should outsource. There are companies that can help you determine your strategy, create content, manage your communities, or manage the entire process.

Splash Media offers a complete turnkey solution that takes all of this off your plate. We might be a good solution for you if you're feeling more overwhelmed than empowered at this point. With our solution, you can be the captain of the ship and let us do all the work for you. We have worked with hundreds of companies in more than 100 different industries, so my guess is you won't throw anything at us we haven't seen before.

Resources

Social Media is an ever-evolving environment and we have resources to help keep you up to date.

- **Our blog** – We post a new article on our blog just about every business day. Monday and Thursday we publish journalistic content about the social media industry in general. Think of it as social media news. Tuesday's are reserved for answering "how to" questions from our community and other useful content for community managers. On Wednesday we post a summary blog of our weekly SplashCast. Finally, on Friday we post a weekly industry recap we call Stories You May Have Missed.

- **SplashCast** – This is our weekly vlog. Each Wednesday we publish something new. You'll find interviews with major brands or with a Splash Media Social Media Manager discussing how they implement social media, as well as interviews with me discussing strategy or current events.

- **Social Media for CEOs Boot Camps** – If you haven't been to one of our free Boot Camps, I encourage you to attend. We have been to over 20 cities and have trained over 20,000 business leaders, making it the most successful social media training event of its kind. We are in a major city most weeks. Visit our website for a current schedule.

- **Facebook and Twitter** – Facebook is a great place to stay connected with the Splash Media team and get a window into the personality and culture of our company. In both platforms we curate useful articles we find that mostly offer tips and tricks for managing social media. Specifically on Twitter we have many handles and hashtags you may want to follow. @SplashMediaLP is our primary handle for all things social media. @SplashCube is our handle for our software platform. My handle is @PaulSlack. With any of our handles, you can ask us questions and we will be quick to respond with our best answer. Our hashtags are #SM4CEOs for general social media information and posts from Boot Camp attendees, and #SplashCube for software-related information.

- **LinkedIn Group** – Our LinkedIn group is called Social Media Boot Camp for CEOs. We have a very active community that is a good mix of social media consultants and business leaders. New discussions are getting started every day. Most of the discussions are initiated by the community and Splash.

- **SplashCube** – SplashCube is a web-based marketing tool

to equip and enable any user with basic computer skills to implement a best-in-class social media marketing strategy for their business. We initially developed SplashCube to help us manage our clients. We needed a tool to make sure we were delivering best-in-class services to all of our clients. We looked at all of the available tools in the market and couldn't find anything that met our needs. Specifically we wanted a tool to help us gauge the overall health of our clients' social media environments, give us business intelligence so we could make good decisions, and provide task management. What we ended up with was something much bigger than we expected. In terms of gauging health, SplashCube uses sophisticated algorithms and literally compares a user's specific social media environment against hundreds of thousands of environments. We also programmed in all of the best practices we have learned from our experience into a recommendation engine so the software can provide specific custom recommended tasks users can implement on a daily basis to perform best-in-class social media marketing. From a task management perspective, this is huge because it's not just managing tasks; it's prescribing best practices and then managing them. This is a tremendous breakthrough compared to all the other tools on the market because SplashCube is the only one that can tell users what to do. This keeps users from ever having to guess what they should be doing within a platform at any moment in time. We also added contextual video help for most of the prescribed tasks, so users can learn as they go.

- **Splash Media U™** – This is our online learning library.

Splash Media U contains hundreds of how-to training videos covering just about every topic you can imagine. From strategic development, to the basics, to advanced tactics, this site is an excellent resource for anyone interested in implementing social media marketing on their own.

- **Mashable** – While this is not a Splash Media site, Mashable is one of the best resources on the web to learn about social media marketing and stay up to date. You will certainly want to follow them and read their content regularly.

Conclusion

As the old cliché goes, "Give a person a fish and you'll feed them for a day. Teach a person how to fish and you'll feed them for a lifetime." This book and the resources Splash Media has made available to you are all about teaching you how to fish. At this point, there should be nothing holding you back from this exciting new era in the world of marketing. Remember, change is inevitable and it always equals opportunity. Don't be fearful of this change but embrace it and become excited about the fact that it's a revolution and as a business owner you can choose to participate in it, rather than become a victim of it.

I want to leave you with one last story to tie everything we have covered in this book together and give you hope that social media marketing is a tool that, when wielded correctly, can provide your business with amazing results. Save Phace, a Splash Media client, is the world's leader in face protection and has three lines of masks; their Sport Utility Mask (SUM), Tactical Masks and the Extreme Face Protector (EFP). Each type of mask satisfies a specific need within the general outdoor recreation industry, paintball and Airsoft industries, as well as the world of welding. Jerry Wright, the owner, is quite gregarious and has a big personality. I remember the day I met him, sitting in my office and thinking to myself how social media would be a home run for him because of his personality and product line. Little did I know how big and how soon.

We started working together in February 2011. During the strategic planning phase, we discovered Save Phace would soon be coming out with a new mask that would revolutionize the welding mask industry. This product would also be their first industrial offering. There hadn't been many changes to the typical welding mask in the past 40 years, and Save Phace was about to alter that by delivering a mask that provides 180 degrees of vision, which is a big improvement from the tiny window commonly found on welding masks. They wanted to use social media not only to enhance their consumer markets but also to help launch Save Phace into the industrial market.

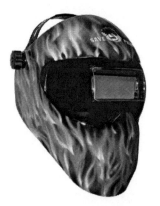 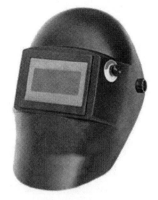

Save Phace welding mask vs. Old school mask

During our initial key phrase research we discovered it would be easy to find sports enthusiasts who are looking for and discussing things like paintball/fishing/outdoor accessories, but it would be more difficult to find their industrial customers. Once we found the right key phrases for their industrial prospects, we discovered that, while it is a much smaller community, they were very active and interested in Save Phace.

As part of our activation strategy, we sent emails to the Save Phace marketing database, inviting customers and prospective customers to join Save Phace's social media communities. We also built a campaign to give away merchandise as their communities grew and hit certain milestones. At one point we had an 8-year-old boy making videos to spread the word about Save Phace to all of his friends. That's word-of-mouth advertising on steroids! Through strategic listening, we were able to find very specific people talking about highly relevant topics of interest to both their consumer and industrial customers.

For every 500 new Facebook fans Save Phace gives away $150 worth of merchandise.

The content strategy involved creating content around what extreme sports enthusiasts and welding professionals were searching for. We created blogs about the best paintball strategies for winning matches, as well as tips for buying face protection. We produced videos to highlight their products and explained the benefits of their revolutionary welding mask.

Social media quickly became a major source of traffic to their website. Today more than 50% of their online orders come from social sites. However, the real story begins with our strategy to tap into the industrial welding market. The focus was to build community with influencers in and around the welding industry, and to lead with value by providing remarkable content and becoming top of mind. One extraordinary example came from Twitter.

Months before the new welding mask was generally available, we began listening for and engaging with welders on Twitter. We ran across a potential customer who was clearly interested in what we had to say. We let him know we had a new welding mask coming out that would revolutionize welding helmets. We stayed in touch and when the mask was ready to be released, he was one of the first to know about it. Since he lived in Italy and didn't want to pay for shipping, he marched right over to his Italian welding supply store and told the owner to start selling the mask. Within a few weeks, Save Phace received a sales lead through the blog from an Italian dealer mentioning he was referred by the potential customer we had connected with on Twitter. That is *really* word-of-mouth advertising on steroids! Not only will this result in one sale, but imagine how many additional welding masks will be sold through this Italian supplier.

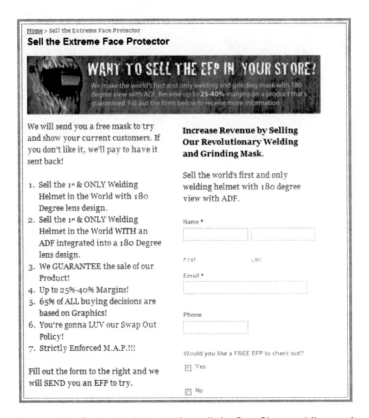

Form on blog for dealers interested to sell the Save Phace welding mask.

Another instance of social media opening doors for Save Phace came from a welding supply dealer in Germany who was out browsing the Internet when he ran across a LinkedIn discussion post we made inside Save Phace's LinkedIn group. What caught his eye was how Save Phace spelled face. He was interested, so he entered the group, saw a discussion we started to promote a recent blog article, read the small caption within the discussion and clicked over to the blog article about the new welding mask.

He read a few more awareness blogs, checked out the website and decided he needed more information, so he filled out the lead capture form on the blog. The same one used by the Italian supplier.

The community manager jumped at the opportunity to let the prospect know Save Phace was excited to talk and set up an appointment for Save Phace's VP of Sales for the next day. Within 24 hours of the initial lead coming through social media, Save Phace had closed the deal to partner with Weldplus. This was a tremendous opportunity for Save Phace as Weldplus has dealers in nearly 10 other countries and holds relationships with several large industrial companies.

Upon further research of Save Phace, Weldplus learned about their other lines and became equally excited about selling them. One connection in particular was derived from the owners of Weldplus and their extensive backgrounds supplying European military forces. The potential for the Save Phace's Tactical mask to be purchased by European militaries is a likely possibility. There are many other examples I could share with you, but these really capture how social media has become a real game-changer for Save Phace.

Save Phace is run by an owner who recognized the world of marketing has changed, and he embraced this change by charging into it with the same gusto he uses to make revolutionary products. He also understood he needed a partner to help Save Phace attack the market because of his limited resources and need for speed. He didn't want to spend months and months trying to figure out social media marketing; he wanted to mine value from the media as quickly as possible. Social media marketing has become an integral part of his business, as he now has a successful industrial product and has expanded into a global supplier. This was accomplished by having a great product, superior customer service, a rock-solid strategy then following the Tactical Wheel and leading with value.

This story shows how a small business leveraged the strategy, principles, and tactics outlined in this book to tap into new markets and achieve amazing growth. Now it's up to you to begin the process for your company. We've come a long way, and I hope I've been a good guide as we have navigated the social media waters together. You now understand how social media relates to business marketing and why it's so important from a consumer perspective. We've spent a lot of time on developing a strategy and discussing best practices and how to use them effectively. Now you are ready to bait your own hook and get down to the business of social media marketing. It has been an honor to be your guide through the chapters of this book. You may not have had as much fun reading it as I did that day on the Sabine River; however, if you will follow the practical steps outlined in this book, you'll receive value that is long lasting.

REFERENCE

SEO Tactics - The Secret Sauce

At the onset of this chapter about SEO 2.0, I have to give you a warning and some advice. This is a long chapter that contains a lot of technical information; it is absolutely crucial that you, as a business owner, gain a firm understanding of SEO. Without the knowledge that will be delivered to you in this chapter, your entire social media success could be in jeopardy. You certainly won't have all the tools you need to be "over the top" successful. To put this in the context of our fishing guide analogy, reading this chapter will be like having to listen to your fishing guide talk about all the fish and different types of habitat and why certain baits will be used—before you even get in the boat. He's walking you through those things because he wants you to have the best possible experience while you're fishing. My mission in this chapter is similar: to give you the information you need to be successful in SEO. You may have to read this section multiple times. That's okay; I promise… it'll be worth it. So hang in there.

I've observed over the past decade or more that many companies and business owners know just enough about search engine optimization to be dangerous. In this chapter, I give you the information you need to build a highly effective SEO strategy that connects with social media to catapult your website, blogs, and videos to the top of the major search engines.

It is important that you avoid some of the irresponsible strategies I've seen companies use in the past, like keyword stuffing. Keyword stuffing is when you take your 100-200 best key phrases and cram them inside various places on all of your web pages. The only thing this method accomplishes is to get you into a lot of trouble with the search engines.

Another way companies try to maximize their SEO is by having an armada of websites, each dedicated to a different key phrase by including that key phrase in the domain name. Then these websites are linked back to the company's primary website to build links or pay a company to generate lots of links to their website. These methods will not cause your website to magically rank well in the search engines. Quite frankly, the search engines are way too sophisticated for such tricks. That's one of the main reasons why Google is the major search engine it is today; they developed sophisticated methods and processes for the way they rank websites that cause most of that kind of trickery to vaporize.

Let's jump in and look and look at the critical components that you will need to learn to make SEO 2.0 work for your business.

How to Conduct Effective Key Phrase Research

Developing a sound SEO 2.0 strategy for your business starts with doing key phrase research. Here is a five-point strategy that will provide you with 99% of what's needed in terms of building a solid SEO 2.0 key phrase analysis for your business. Remember, we need to begin with the end in mind. That's why key phrase research is the very first thing you should do. We want to learn what those words and phrases are that potential customers will type into major sites like Google, to understand more about our industry or to formulate their buying criteria.

1. **Initial Research**

    Talk to your sales reps and ask them, "What do you think our customers or potential customers might type into a search engine if they were looking for us or our products?"

You can also talk to current clients or perspective clients and ask them that same question. Spend time looking at your competitors' websites. Once you get a few key phrases you think are relevant, search these phrases in Google to see what companies are popping up in the results. Take note of the key phrases they have in the hyperlink in Google and even the descriptive text underneath. Go visit their website and look at some of the copy and the words they're including in their headlines. Pay close attention to the way they describe their products and services. Take thorough notes.

2. **Google-Related Searches**

   Once you have what you feel is a pretty good starting point, what I call a seed list of phrases you think represent what you're customers are looking for, type those into Google one at a time. Then, on the left side of a Google search results page, click on Related Searches. This will give you suggestions from Google that are related to the key phrase you typed in. This tool provides great intelligence on how your potential customers are looking for the products and services that you provide. Google uses sophisticated algorithms to analyze search behavior and their related searches suggestions come from how users refine their searches as they look for information. Notice in the following image when Related Searches is clicked, Google provides key phrase suggestions below the search bar.

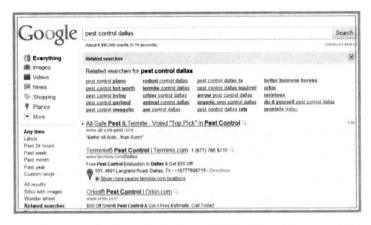

Click on related searches in the left column. This will provide suggested key phrases under the search bar

3. Key Phrase Spreadsheet

Once you get the suggestions from Google right below the search bar, copy and paste those words into a spreadsheet. Repeat the process until you've gone through all the different key phrases that were on your notepad. Now you have a very comprehensive list of phrases that will be extremely relevant to your potential customers.

4. Key Phrases into Buckets

You'll notice there are some key phrases that are very similar because you may have multiple products and some of the key phrases are related to one product while others are related to another. Break those up and put them into multiple tabs in your spreadsheet. You should have a tab in the spreadsheet for each grouping or bucket of key phrases, and each tab should probably have around 15-20 different phrases at a minimum.

Once you have the terms grouped into the different buckets, you have what you need to build a content strategy. I would encourage you to take these key phrases and match them up with the list of over 50 different headline ideas in the Appendix of this book. This will give you topic ideas for great content that's useful and beneficial to your target audience. To help you come up with the different topics of interest for your target market and how you can leverage those topics across many social media platforms, I have included a content plan in the resources section of the Splash Media website. Remember, optimizing your content is critical. So when you come up with a topic that you think would be really relevant and useful for your target audience, you don't want that topic to exist in just one social media channel. For instance, if you create a video for YouTube, you could turn the audio of that video into a podcast at iTunes and you could write a summary of that video and turn it into a blog post. In essence, one idea or one topic can actually become multiple pieces of content. The free downloadable content plan I've posted on the Splash Media website can walk you through how to maximize your content to reach your customer on many levels.

Is your head spinning yet? This is a lot of information and you're not even halfway through the chapter. To help make this easier to digest, I have a couple of videos for you on how to develop a key phrase analysis and put together a solid content plan. Visit www.splashmedia.com/resources to gain access.

Fasten your seatbelt because it's about to get more technical as we explore what to do with these two items. By using our begin-with-the-end-in-mind approach and leveraging your key phrase research to build your content strategy, you will set your company up for SEO 2.0 success.

On-the-Page Optimization

Now that you have your key phrases and content strategy in place, let's look at how to optimize the content you produce. With regard to on-the-page optimization, you need to understand that search engines are like detectives. As you might imagine, a detective is looking for clues. When search engines review the content you produce, they look for clues to understand the nature of the content. In most cases, it won't be a person reviewing your content but rather a specialized algorithm commonly known as a search engine spider or crawler. The art of on-the-page SEO is to first understand where those clue areas are best located. The good news is they exist on every single page on the web, regardless of whether it's a web page on your website, an article on your blog, or a video. Those clue areas will exist in the same places every time. You also need to make sure the targeted key phrases for a piece of content exist in those optimal clue areas.

Search engines also have a web page paradigm rather than a website paradigm, which means they review individual pieces of content rather than look at a website or a blog in its entirety. Therefore, the search engines don't see your blog as one environment that should be ranked for a set of key phrases; they see individual blog articles that should be ranked for the topic of each article. When you optimize content, find the two or three most relevant key phrases and use those in the clue areas only. Take the less-is-more approach and don't try to do too much with one piece of content. This only confuses the search engines.

Another key element to understand is search engines rate prominence from left to right and top to bottom on a page. When you start to explore these clue areas, remember the things you put toward the left will be considered more important than items on the right side of your pages. For example, in a headline your key phrase should be the first words of that headline, rather than the last words because the search engines will understand them to be the most important. The same is true if you put the key phrase early in the content rather than only in the last paragraph.

These clues exist within three key areas: page content, architecture, and source code. These key areas work together like a three-legged stool. Content is the words you can visibly see in a blog article, on a web page, or in a video. Architecture is the way; you name pages and files and link pages together. Source code is what's under the hood, if you will, which also includes clues for the search engines. So let's take a look at each one of these in detail.

1. **Content**

   On web pages and in blog articles content is the visible copy you can see. If you're looking at a web page, content is the copy or blog article. The same is true for your tweets or status updates; content is the copy you can actually copy, cut and paste right from the web document and put it in another location. For blog articles and web pages, it's best that your copy be about 200-300 words on each page. This seems to work the best in terms of getting search engine rankings. That doesn't mean you shouldn't have a blog that is 500 words of copy or a video summary that's only 100 words; I've seen 200-300 words work well with search engines. If you have a blog with a thousand words, I recommend breaking that one long blog into a series of two shorter blogs that will run in succession.

   With regard to on-the-page optimization, it's important to remember that less is more. When you're working key phrases into a page of content, don't try to work all of them in all of the time. The good news about the strategy I'm laying out in this book is you'll be producing content every week (blog) and every month (video) through social media, so you don't have to accomplish all of your SEO goals all at once with one piece of content. You can break those key phrases up and work on a couple every single week and over time you'll have great exposure for all of your different key phrases. If you try to do it all at once, you'll actually defeat the purpose because you're confusing the search engines. Remember, they're like detectives and they're trying to understand what your web pages and blog articles are about. The minute you introduce too many key phrases into a document in these clue areas, you're confusing them.

Your goal is to target no more than two or three very closely related phrases on any one item of content. From those two to three phrases, select a primary key phrase, the one that's the most important to you. For example, if you're writing a blog about accounting software, your key phrases might be "small business accounting software, "accounting software for small business" and "accounting software providers" because those are all closely related. However, on the same piece of content, you wouldn't try to optimize "financial software," "payroll software" or "bookkeeping software" because even though they're similar, they're not closely related. You can do a future blog article about financial software or payroll software. The key point is to produce a steady diet of content over time, so you don't have the burden of trying to make a document rank for too many things.

Be sure to include the primary key phrase in the headline of the document. Search engines obviously assume words in the headline are a key clue regarding the content. It's best if that phrase is the first words of the headline. For example: "Small Business Accounting Software: What's New in 2011." The primary key phrase should also get worked into the first sentence of the first paragraph and one or two more times within the other paragraphs. The other key phrases should be sprinkled in throughout the copy.

2. **Architecture**

   Architecture is the second leg of the stool. You can optimize your architecture in four ways.

   Page names with key phrase in URL: One of the first things you can do is make sure the page names have your primary key phrase in the URL structure. For example, if you published a blog article on small business accounting software, you want to make sure the name of that page is XYZCompanyBlog.com/small_business_accounting_software. Most blogging software will automatically assign the specific URL (permalink) based on the headline of the blog, which you can change. From the headline example I gave in the content section above, this would mean your blogging software would automatically create the URL XYZCompanyBlog.com/small_business_accounting_software _what's_ new_ in_ 2011, which is entirely too long for a page name. Therefore, I would shorten the page name to just XYZCompanyBlog.com/small_business_accounting_software before you publish the blog article.

   Have a sitemap: Another key point of developing good architecture is to have a sitemap. A sitemap, as you can see here in this example, is a web page on your site that acts as a table of contents page of all the different pages in your site, and it includes hyperlinks to the individual pages. Hyperlinks are those links that have text in them and they are important clues for the search engines. A sitemap page is an all-you-can-eat buffet of clues.

Create XML Sitemap: The XML Sitemap is actually the preferred way to submit your site to the search engines. It's an XML feed of the content in your site and blog that's generated by using Google Webmaster Tools software. Go to http://www.google.com/webmasters/ and sign up for an account. Register your website or your blog and they will give you a tool that will spider through your site and create an XML sitemap that you can then feed back to Google. You'll want to do this with your blog and website because by setting up an account, you're agreeing to abide by their terms and conditions and agreeing not to spam or trick them into making your website rank for something irrelevant. Websites that have these XML sitemaps tend to get visited more by search engine crawlers and rank better than other sites.

Link between pages on your website: Using hyperlinks with key-phrase-rich anchor tags to link between pages is another important clue. A great example of this is Wikipedia. Wikipedia tends to rank very high for just about every key phrase that you can imagine. If you look at a Wikipedia page, you'll notice there are a lot of hyperlinks on those pages with a related key phrase linked to another page. This is one of the main reasons Wikipedia shows up in search results. You don't have to be as over the top as Wikipedia is, but you want to take that same approach in your blogs and on your website because you want to drop clues and make it easy for the search engine to find all the pages in your site and understand the relationship between those pages.

Here is an example of an active call to action inside a blog to drive leads for free estimate.

The above display is an example of anchor tags that shows how one particular financial accounting software blog article can link your visitor to another article using a hyperlink. You put a link on that particular page, not to benefit that page, but rather to benefit the page it's linking to about financial accounting software because (1) you're making it easy for the search engines to find that page and (2) you're dropping a clue along the way.

Include at least one link in your blog to another related blog and one link to a page on your website. Find a key phrase that's in your current blog that would naturally relate to another blog or page on your site. Don't just think in terms of linking to your home page. Instead, link to deeper, relevant, important content within your site, using anchor tags to drive people to important information or a call to action.

Specifically as it relates to blog articles, you have two additional architecture opportunities with your blog that you don't have on your website today— Categorization and Tagging. When you create a blog article you have an opportunity to select a category for the article as well as tag for it. These are both very important clue opportunities for the search engines. Follow this less-is-more approach and only categorize a blog in a keyword-rich category that's very relevant to the topic. For instance, if you're an accounting software company, I probably wouldn't have categories like *software reviews* or *software articles;* I'd be more descriptive, such as *accounting* software reviews or *accounting* software articles.

With regard to tagging, the same less-is-more approach is best. Tag only key phrases that are relevant. If you selected three key phrases for a particular article, you should only tag it with those three key phrases because those are the search engine clues. Your goal is to be very clear to the search engines and communicate to them as effectively as you can. A very common mistake in the world of blog optimization is an overuse of tagging. At the end of the day, tagging is a form of keyword stuffing, which never accomplishes anything good for the publisher of the content.

3. **Source Code**

    How do you find your source code? When you are on a particular page of your website, right-click over your document, and then click on View Source. Your source code for that page will actually appear and there are some key clue areas within that source code as well.

    When search engines crawl through the content posted on your blog and website they store a copy of your source code in their database. When someone does a search at a major site like Google, the search engine scours through all the data gathered from source code files in their database to find the most relevant content. That's why it's really important that the key phrases you are targeting for optimizing a web page or blog article are found inside the source code.

    Within the source code the most important area for optimization is what is called "meta data." You've probably heard the terms "meta data" or "meta tags" before. Meta data is simply data about data. Any electronic file that has ever been created has meta data. If you've ever hovered over a Word document with your mouse and seen the little pop-up box that shows the last time something was modified, you are seeing meta data. Web pages, blogs, video, podcasts and any type of content you can produce electronically, will have meta data because it is an electronic file. Inside of meta data there are meta tags, which is where you're going to be able to add key phrases in the source code.

There are three important tags that you need to be aware of: Title, Description and Alternative Text for Images.

Title Tag: This is the most important of the tags and one of the most critical optimization elements that you have when it comes to on-the-page optimization. Your Title Tag is meant to be the title of your document. Often people will use the headline as the title tag and that's fine. It should contain six to eight words and have the primary key phrase toward the left side.

Here's what **not** to do with the Title Tag, which is a very common mistake. Do not put your company name in the Title Tag. Unless you're a major brand, like Kleenex or Tupperware, it doesn't really make sense for you to include your name in the Title Tag because nobody knows who you are; you would be much better off to use that valuable real estate for key phrases more than anything else. If you must include your company name place it at the end of the title tag.

It's important to understand that what you put in a Title Tag is visible to your visitors. In the following example, you're going to see whatever you put in the Title Tag is what the search engines are going to use as the hyperlink inside of their search result to that page.

Description Tag: This is a 20-30 word description about the content of that page. Think of it in terms of being a brief summary of that page; however, from a search engine optimization perspective it's important because this is a place where you'll be able to include synonyms and derivatives for your targeted key phrases. Description Tags are also seen by visitors because the descriptive text shows up in the search result page right underneath the hyperlink.

You'll want to use transitional statements in your Descriptions Tags to easily add these synonyms, derivatives, and other descriptive words that you're trying to target. Take a look at the following example.

"<u>Small business accounting software provider</u> discusses how companies in <u>real estate</u>, <u>home construction</u>, and <u>pest control</u> can benefit from <u>accounting packages</u> like <u>QuickBooks</u>, <u>Sage</u> and <u>Netsuite</u>."

Everything that's underlined in this example is a key phrase. Even though the primary key phrase might have been small business accounting software, we're trying to work in other synonyms or derivatives that might help with search engine results.

Alternative Text for Images: Alternative Text is what you see when you hover over an image with your mouse and a pop-up box appears containing words about the image. I recommend that any web content you create, whether it's a web page or a blog article, have images contained in the content and you add alternative context to that image. The key to utilizing Alternative Text correctly for SEO is to use only one key phrase to describe the picture and make sure it is relevant to the image as well as relevant to the content on the page.

That covers all the things you need to do on a particular piece of content to get it to rank well in the search engines. Remember this is half the battle. You will also have to work within the World Wide Web to drop clues and properly influence the search engines to generate the desired search results for your business.

Off-the-Page Optimization

Off-the-page optimization has to do with building inbound links to your website. This is the Holy Grail of SEO 2.0, and thanks to social search you can better leverage the power of inbound links to help improve your ranking in the search engines. Back in the days when it was just Yahoo!, AltaVista and Lycos, those search engines paid no attention at all to what other people thought about your website. When Google came on the scene, they added the element of on-the-page optimization *plus* what other people think about your web pages, and they measure this by how many other web pages have links to your content. Think of it as a popularity contest; the more links you have, the better your website will rank. Over time those algorithms have become more sophisticated and it's not just how many sites are pointing to you; it's also about how important those sites are that point to you.

The good news is search engines now consider social media content important and highly relevant. For instance, if you get a link from someone else's blog to your blog, or from a highly regarded social media network like Twitter or Facebook, this will help all of your content rank better.

Link Building Basics

There are lots of ways to build links to your content on your own that will help you with off-the-page optimization.

1. Become intentional about linking articles in your blog to pages on your website using anchor tags to relevant content within your website.

2. Create a summary blog to promote your YouTube videos

and include the video in the blog. Therefore, when you drop links to your video in social sites like Twitter or Facebook, you are actually dropping links back to your blog summary where users can watch the video. This builds links for your blog versus building links for YouTube.

3. Create a Facebook note that is a summary of a blog with a link to the blog from Facebook.

4. Share your blog or video summary within LinkedIn groups that you have joined. LinkedIn groups are crawled quite a bit by the search engines, so if you start a discussion with links to this type of content you will build link popularity. You can also comment or contribute to a discussion that's already going on and provide relevant information by dropping a link to your content.

5. Thoroughly complete your social media profiles. Be as complete as possible when filling out all of your social media profiles and make sure you drop in links to your website and blog.

6. Create a steady diet of online press releases. Try to do at least one press release every month and upload it to a submission site such as PRWeb.com. At the time of this writing, their entry level per-submission rate is $80, which will garner you plenty of play in search. What's great about press releases is that you'll show up in search engine news within 24 hours and you'll start showing up in search results for related keywords in two weeks or less. They also get picked up and published in other social media sites, which is great because a lot of blogs are using press releases to backfill their blog content if they believe

it's useful to their readers. If you write a press release that's fully optimized, it can be picked up hundreds or thousands of times, mainly in other people's blogs. If you include links to your website within the press release, you not only will create a lot of exposure in other blogs but also a lot of links back to your own environment.

Commenting

Look for blog articles that contain phrases from your key phrase list. You can do this by simply typing these phrases into Google and then clicking on the Blog link on the left column of the search results page. Once you've found a few articles, start leaving comments and dropping a link to a relevant blog article or website. Avoid being self-promotional right out of the gate, or commenting too often. Do not start by commenting on somebody's blog and saying, "Boy, that's a great article. I've written an article just like that in my blog. Here's the link to it." That's not very effective and you're certainly not leading with value. Join the conversation first by becoming a voice within that blog by sharing your knowledge regarding the blog topic. After you've done that for a while, you will be in a position to share relevant information you have on your blog, to which you can drop in a link within the comment section of that environment.

Broadcasting

Broadcasting is another way of building link popularity. I recommend every single time you create social media content, plan on promoting it by tweeting two to three times and maybe more, depending on your industry. You'll have to experiment with it. A good starting point would be to promote it via Twitter at least two to three times and swap out the key phrases that you targeted for that article in each of your tweets. For example, one tweet might be "small business accounting software" as the key phrase and the next tweet might be "accounting software for a small business."

Link Baiting

Link baiting is intentionally creating content that people will want to share. They'll most often share it by dropping a link to your content within their social media environments. People will share your content if they find it interesting and relevant. The first step to creating link bait content is it must be compelling and unique. In other words, you need to have a fresh perspective.

This is similar to creating a video in hopes that it will go viral. In some cases it is like trying to win the lottery. You don't really know what your chances are of going viral; you just know the odds are not in your favor. At most you want 10% to 20% of the content you create with this kind of link baiting viral idea in mind. You'll be surprised at the things that go viral and create a lot of link traffic.

Here are examples of the types of things that tend to be good candidates for link baiting.

Info-graphics: This is when you take data and create a graphic that is not readily available on other sites. People will link to it and share it for the benefit of their audience.

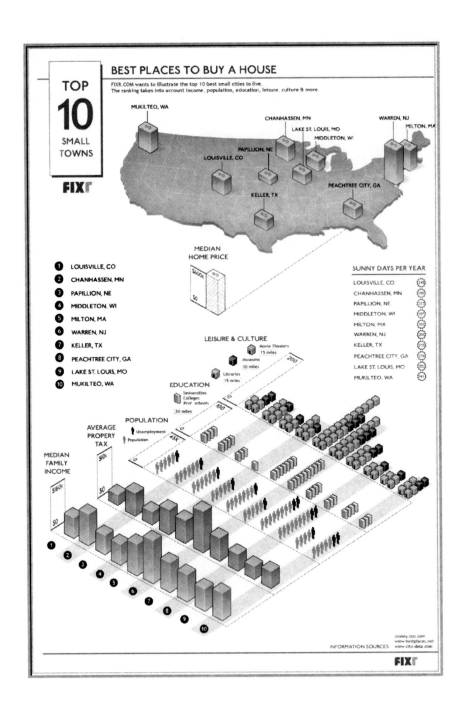

Polls or surveys: You can go out and survey all the environments your clients participate in and put together a summary report on the trends you're seeing. You can solicit polls from your followers and then produce those results, inviting your audience to see how they responded relative to other participants.

Controversial content: This is one of my favorites. Every industry has issues you can flip upside down and take the counterpoint on and that tends to create good inbound links.

Awards: You can create your own award for just about anything. For example, you can award top vendors, partners, or industry bloggers. Believe me, the winning companies or bloggers will link to your content because they'll want to promote themselves by sharing it with their audience.

Look inside something new. Finally, you might consider taking apart a brand new product related to your industry and writing an article on what you find on the inside. I remember when the first Apple iPhone hit the streets; there were lots of articles published regarding what technology Apple was using on the inside.

You made it through the thickest chapter in the book. My guess is you will be referring back to these pages again and again as you work on developing social media content that will not only please your audience but the search engines as well. The reward will be high rankings, lots of traffic, and more friends, fans, followers, and most importantly customers. I will end this chapter and each of the subsequent chapters with Pro Tips that will be an easy reference for key points made within each chapter.

Social Rules – SEO Tactics – The Secret Sauce:

Rule #78   A steady diet of search-engine-friendly social media content (blogs and videos) is the best way to generate search engine traffic.

Rule #79: Begin with the end in mind and use Google Related Searches to come up with the best key phrases for your business.

Rule #80: Create an XML sitemap and register it with Google Webmaster Tools.

Rule #81: Link pages within your website and blog to each other using keyword-rich anchor text.

Rule #82: Use key phrases in Headlines, titles, descriptions, and page names.

Rule #83: Off-the-page optimization is just as important as on-the-page optimization, and you need to be intentional about building links to your content within the World Wide Web.

APPENDIX

Chapter 1: Social Media Revolution

Sources for Social Media Facts and Stats:

http://www.hubspot.com/Portals/53/docs/resellers/reports/state_of_inbound_marketing.pdf

http://www.webdesignerdepot.com/2011/01/too-many-blogs/

http://blog.twitter.com/2011/03/numbers.html

http://www.digitalbuzzblog.com/facebook-statistics-stats-facts-2011/

http://www.kenburbary.com/2011/03/facebook-demographics-revisited-2011-statistics-2/

http://answers.yahoo.com/question/index?qid=20100728222055AA0v1Pj

Chapter 2: What is Social Media Marketing?

Seth Godin, Permission Marketing (Simon & Schuster, 1999)

Dale Carnegie, How to Win Friends and Influence People (Simon & Schuster, 1936)

Chapter 7: Listening

The most common Boolean Searches we use at Splash Media:

1. Target By Occupation (Gives you a list of all the users that have the word "attorney" in their title (username and/or real name)

    a. intitle:"attorney * on twitter" site:twitter.comTarget by Bio

2. Target by Bio (Looks for a job title of target audience in your bio section on Twitter)

    a. intext:"bio * Occupation" site:twitter.com

3. Target By Keyword (Searches by Keyword or "Key Phrase")

    a. intext:" keyword" site:twitter.com

    b. intext:" keyword" site:linkedin.com/groups

4. Target By Location (Looks at Twitter Handle and Bio for Attorney and the reads)

5. (intitle:"attorney * on twitter" OR intext:"bio * attorney") intext:"location * TX" site:twitter.com

Chapter 9: Broadcasting

Holidays to include in your Editorial Calendar for scheduled broadcasting.

January

- 1 January – New Year's Day
- Martin Luther King, Jr. Day (3rd Monday of January, traditionally 15 Jan.)
- Community Manager Appreciation Day (4th Monday of January)

February

- 2 February – Groundhog Day

- 12 February – Lincoln's Birthday
- 14 February – Valentine's Day
- 17 February - Random Acts of Kindness Day
- Presidents Day (officially George Washington's Birthday; 3rd Monday of February, traditionally 22 Feb.)

March

- Fat Tuesday (always the day before Lent starts)
- Ash Wednesday (Christian; movable; First day of the 40-day Lent Season – ending Palm Sunday)
- 17 March – St. Patrick's Day (Originating in Ireland)
- Vernal Equinox (based on sun)
- National Corndog Day (1st Saturday of the NCAA Men's Division 1 Basketball Championship)
- First day of Passover (Jewish; movable based on Jewish calendar)
- 30 March – National Doctors' Day (always on 30 March)

April

- 1 April – April Fools' Day
- 16 April – Foursquare Day or 4sqDay
- National Dark-Sky Week (during the week of the new moon in April)
- Good Friday (Christian; Friday before Easter)
- Easter Sunday (Christian; movable; Sunday after first full moon during spring)

- Easter Monday (Christian; Monday after Easter)
- Patriots' Day/Marathon Monday (New England and Wisconsin only)(3rd Monday of April)
- 22 April – Earth Day
- 26 April - National Paper Airplane Day
- 27 April - Administrative Professionals Day
- Arbor Day (last Friday of April)

May

- 4 May – Star Wars Day
- National Day of Prayer (United States Congress, when people are asked "to turn to God in prayer and meditation". 1st Thursday of May)
- Mother's Day (2nd Sunday of May)
- Armed Forces Day (3rd Saturday in May)

June

- Pentecost Sunday (Christian; 49 days after Easter)
- 30 May – Memorial Day (last Monday of May, traditionally 30 May)
- 14 June – Flag Day
- Father's Day (3rd Sunday of June)
- Summer Solstice (based on sun)

July

- 4 July – Independence Day
- International Free Hugs Day (1st Saturday of July)

August
- August 5 - International Beer Day
- International Bacon Day (Saturday before Labor Day)

September
- Labor Day (first Monday of September)
- Rosh Hashanah (Jewish; moveable, based on Jewish calendar)
- 11 September – Patriot Day
- 17 September – Constitution Day – Celebration of the ratification of the Constitution of the United States.
- 19 September - International Talk Like a Pirate Day
- 22 September – Hobbit Day
- Yom Kippur (Jewish, moveable, 9 days after first day of Rosh Hashanah)
- First day of Sukkot (Jewish; moveable, 14 days after Rosh Hashanaah)
- Autumnal equinox (based on sun)
- Simchat Torah (Jewish; moveable, 22 days after Rosh Hashanah)
- Ask a Stupid Question Day (Last school day in September)

October
- Columbus Day (2nd Monday of October, traditionally 12 Oct.)
- 16 October – Boss' Day

- 31 October – Halloween

November

- 1 November – All Saints Day (Christian)
- 11 November – Veterans Day
- Thanksgiving (4th Thursday of November)
- Black Friday (The day after Thanksgiving)
- Cyber Monday (The Monday after Black Friday)

December

- First day of Hanukkah (Jewish; moveable, based on Jewish calendar)
- 7 December – Pearl Harbor Remembrance Day
- Winter Solstice (based on sun)
- 24 December - Christmas Eve (Christian)
- 25 December – Christmas Day (Christian)
- 26 December – First day of Kwanzaa (Kwanzaa is celebrated until 1 January)
- 31 December – New Year's Eve

Chapter 10: Developing Content

Headline Suggestions: Use this list along with your key phrase analysis to come up with topics for your content plan.

1. Pros and cons of [Key Phrase]
2. How to [Key Phrase]
3. "XYZ Product" goes head to head against "Competitor

Product"

4. Latest trends for [Key Phrase]
5. [Key Phrase] Demystified or De-mystifying[Key Phrase]
6. Top (10/50/100) reasons to [Key Phrase]
7. Top (10/50/100) things to do before [Key Phrase]
8. Top (10/50/100) things to avoid when/before [Key Phrase]
9. Why [unique selling proposition] is critical for your business/family/piece of mind
10. A beginners guide to [Key Phrase]
11. [Key Phrase] 201. Taking [Key Phrase] to the next level
12. History of [Key Phrase]
13. A more effective way to [Key Phrase]
14. Little know secrets about [Key Phrase]
15. [Key Phrase]: What's different in 2011
16. [Key Phrase] vs. [Key Phrase]top (5/10/100) differences
17. [Key Phrase]: Most comment mistakes to avoid
18. Top stories for [Key Phrase] (a roundup of articles/blogs within the industry for the month /quarter/year).
19. Little know ways to [Key Phrase]
20. The secret of successful [Key Phrase]
21. The secret of protecting [Key Phrase]
22. How to get the most out of [Key Phrase]
23. Get rid of [Key Phrase] one and for all

24. How every mom/dad/CEO should deal with [Key Phrase]

25. 5 quick tips to get over/rid of [Key Phrase] in your home/company

26. What everyone should know about [Key Phrase]

27. 5/10/100 things your [Key Phrase] won't tell you

28. 5/10/100 simple steps/tricks/techniques for maximizing/reducing/learning/utilizing [Key Phrase]

29. Pros and Cons of [Key Phrase]

30. Get a bigger, faster [Key Phrase]

31. The truth about [Key Phrase]

32. Why [Key Phrase] is better/worse than [Key Phrase]

33. Who/What is [Key Phrase]

34. 5/10/100 Things You Didn't Know about [Key Phrase]

35. 5/10/100 Reasons to Hate [Key Phrase]

36. 5/10/100 Amazing Blogs about [Key Phrase]

37. 5/10/100 Secrets about [Key Phrase]

38. How Does [Key Phrase] Work?

39. How to be Great at [Key Phrase]

40. 5/10/100 [Key Phrase] Myths Exposed

41. [Key Phrase] Myths vs. the Facts

42. 5/10/100 Deadly [Key Phrase] Mistakes You Might Be Making

43. 5/10/100 Shocking Facts about [Key Phrase]

44. 5/10 Questions to Ask about [Key Phrase]

45. Everything You Know about [Key Phrase] is Wrong

46. The Science behind [Key Phrase]

47. 10 [Key Phrase] Experts to Follow on Twitter

48. 5/10[Key Phrase]Rules You Should Follow

49. 5/10 Cool [Key Phrase] Tricks You Aren't Using

50. Get Rid of [Key Phrase]with [Key Phrase]

Chapter 12: Facebook

Quantcast study link: http://www.quantcast.com/www.facebook.com

Chapter 16: YouTube

BusinessWeek

Additional video sites to share your content:

1. Download.com and CNET TV – www.cnettv.com
2. MetaCafe – www.metacafe.com
3. Revver – www.revver.com
4. BlipTV – www.blip.tv
5. Daily Motion – www.dailymotion.com
6. Vimeo – www.vimeo.com Paul Slack

ABOUT THE AUTHOR: **PAUL SLACK**

Remember the days of Lycos and AltaVista? Paul Slack does; he cut his teeth as a web marketing consultant during the dawn of the Internet revolution in the 1990s. As new digital technologies have changed the global business environment ever since, Paul has been able to put them into practice for clients.

In 2000, Paul used his expertise in search engine marketing and search engine optimization to found WebDex Media Group, a Dallas-based firm that provided strategic planning, SEM/SEO, web-based lead generation, online public relations and customer acquisition programs.

Paul and WebDex also quickly became expert in the use of social media tools to help connect clients to customers—an effort that continues with the acquisition of WebDex by Splash Media in 2010. Since the merger, Paul has helped Splash Media become one of the fastest growing, most experienced social media marketing firms in the country.

In early 2012 Paul added the title of President of Splash Media U, taking the reins of his company's social media marketing training and certification program. He is also in demand as a featured speaker on social media and search engine marketing.

To connect with Paul via social media:

Twitter: @PaulSlack

LinkedIn: www.linkedin.com/in/paulslack

CPSIA information can be obtained at www.ICGtesting.com
Printed in the USA
LVOW060256150512

281650LV00004B/4/P